Reading all types
of writing

RETHINKING READING

Series Editor: L. John Chapman
School of Education, The Open University

Current titles:

Reading all types of writing

The importance of genre and register for reading development

ALISON B. LITTLEFAIR

Open University Press
Milton Keynes · Philadelphia

Open University Press
Celtic Court
22 Ballmoor
Buckingham MK18 1XW

and
1900 Frost Road, Suite 101
Bristol, PA 19007, USA

First Published 1991

British Library Cataloguing in Publication Data

Littlefair, Alison B.
Reading all types of writing: the importance of genre and
register for reading development. – (Rethinking reading).
1. Great Britain. Schools. Curriculum subjects. Reading.
Teaching
I. Title II. Series
428.4071041

ISBN 0-335-09278-0
ISBN 0-335-09277-2 (pbk)

Library of Congress Cataloging-in-Publication Data

Littlefair, Alison B. (Alison Barbara), 1934-
Reading all types of writing: the importance of genre and
register for reading development/Alison B. Littlefair.
    p.   cm. -- (Rethinking reading)
Includes bibliographical references (p.   ) and index.
1. Reading (Elementary) 2. Reading (Secondary) 3. Reading-
Language experience approach. 4. Reading comprehension.
I. Title. II. Series.
LB1573.L49 1990
428.4--dc20   90-39817
                                                               CIP

Typeset by Burns & Smith Limited, Derby
Printed in Great Britain

For Reg, Kim, Michael and David

Contents

List of figures and tables

List of tables

List of figures

Why this book has been written

Many books have been written by distinguished teachers and scholars about the teaching and learning of reading. Yet, I am aware from my own teaching experience and from continuing reports of older pupils' inadequate reading abilities, that many pupils do not develop flexible reading skills and all too often almost cease to use reading as either a means for enjoyment or for learning.

It seems timely to discuss ways in which we might help pupils develop their reading ability as they proceed through primary and secondary school. Clearly, pupils do not develop their reading ability simply by becoming older. Young junior school pupils who have come to enjoy reading stories cannot necessarily transfer this reading ability into an ability to read for information. Yet, we all too easily present these pupils with non-fiction books and ask them to search for information and then to write about it.

On the other hand, we often despair that most new entrants into the secondary school are unable to read independently from subject texts across the curriculum. Lunzer and Gardner (1979) revealed evidence that the secondary school pupils they observed read very little. In fact, they spoke of 'a retreat from print' occurring in secondary schools.

There is no real evidence to suggest that this situation has improved. Recent research (Chapman 1987) has shown that the reading ability of many pupils actually decreases as they go through the secondary school. My own research (Littlefair 1988) implies that most readers, however skilled, seem to find some problem in understanding different types of writing. Whatever the age range of pupils we teach or whatever our subject speciality, we are concerned in some way with pupils' reading. As pupils proceed through school, they increasingly read for learning and for enrichment of experience. We cannot assume that these reading purposes will automatically be managed by the majority of pupils. Our common concern is, therefore, how we are to go about teaching pupils something about the varieties of writing they will meet without making reading into a sterile exercise.

To begin with, we might consider how readers of varying abilities develop awareness of the different ways in which texts are written. A purpose of this book is to describe how some junior school readers and some secondary school readers seem to develop this kind of awareness and why this development is so important for them as competent readers.

An important purpose of writing this book is to present a more linguistically informed view of teaching and learning to read. Perhaps because reading is about understanding written text, the process has been looked at for decades from a cognitive point of view. Cognition is an integral part of the reading process but the linguistic aspect is equally an integral part of language learning.

So this book is also concerned with presenting new thinking which provides us with insights into language teaching and learning for it looks closely at the way in which language is used. Much of this research is comparatively new and is not well known in this country. These language studies are largely the work of a group of linguists and teachers in Australia who are developing the ideas of Michael Halliday. Halliday is a leading member of the school of systemic linguists who are concerned with the dynamics of language as it is used rather than an analytical study of how grammar is acquired.

In this country, Halliday is well known for his direction in the 1960s of the Schools Council Programme in Linguistics and English teaching. You may well be familiar with *Breakthrough to Literacy* (Mackay *et al.* 1970) which is an important and influential result of that work. Another result was *Language in Use* (Doughty *et al.* 1971) which is a scheme of language work for secondary schools.

When Halliday took the Chair of Linguistics at Sydney University, much of the thinking about how linguistics might inform the teaching and learning of language shifted to the southern hemisphere. In 1976, Halliday became consultant to the Australian Curriculum Development Centre's Language Development Project which has been described as 'one of the largest Applied Linguistics programmes in the world' (Martin *et al* n.d.: 58). Language and education conferences are arranged where teachers and linguists meet and discuss matters which interest them both. From these discussions has come, and still comes, much that helps us to understand how we might teach and our pupils learn about language. In particular, there is great discussion about the different types of language we use for different purposes. Another way of referring to this kind of language variety is to use the terms, *register* and *genre*. These ideas are often referred to as *genre theory*.

It is these linguistic concepts which are implicit in the new legislation about teaching English in Great Britain. Knowledge of these concepts illuminates much of what both Kingman and Cox have had to say about the teaching and learning of language (Littlefair 1990). The concepts give us an opportunity to look again at reading development and to see ways in which we over-estimate pupils' ability to develop into independent readers as they proceed through junior and secondary schools.

More specifically, here is a linguistic approach to the teaching of reading for, if we are to implement the National Curriculum with understanding and flexibility, then we need to be fairly explicitly aware of the language concepts it implies. Most teachers realize this point but find language study itself rather daunting. Linguistics may seem to be an academic study which is quite remote from the demands of the classroom and, indeed, from many teachers' own education and training. The approach to linguistics described here offers a practical way of understanding far more about language and real possibility of using this knowledge in the classroom.

There is no suggestion in this book that teachers should dissect different types of texts and teach isolated features of language. However, as teachers, we will have enormous advantage if we are sufficiently aware of the way in which authors use language, so that we can anticipate readers' difficulties and intervene in the reading process appropriately. There is no formula for this kind of help. Rather, such knowledge of how language is used will become part of our professional expertise as will the decision when to use that knowledge to assist individual readers as they progress through school and attempt to attain the proposal for attainment in reading set out in *English for Ages 5 to 16* (DES 1989), 16.21:

> the development of the ability to read, understand and respond to all types of writing, as well as the development of information retrieval strategies for the purposes of study.

How to read this book

Readers will have different reasons for selecting this book. Some will look for practical help in the classroom as they begin to cope with the demands of the National Curriculum. Their emphasis will be on the practical application of the ideas which I am presenting. Others will wish to extend their knowledge about the way in which language works and will be interested to find out more about current thinking in Australia. Because of this difference in emphasis in readers' purposes, I have had some difficulty in deciding the order of the chapters. The problem is somewhat resolved by giving a brief description of the chapters and suggesting those which these different readers will find most helpful.

Some readers will wish to read only a brief description of register and genre which they will find in Chapter 2. If you are interested to find out more about these linguistic concepts, and about the ideas of the systemic linguists working in Australia, I suggest you complement Chapter 2 by reading the Technical Appendix.

You may be particularly interested in considering how register and genre relate to the reading recommendations for the National Curriculum. Chapter 1 looks at a practical way of categorizing the different types of writing which have so far been recommended in the National Curriculum for pupils to read. This chapter also introduces the idea of linking forms of genres with authors' purposes. These different categories, or genres, have some common characteristic features of register which are described in Chapter 3. This chapter describes something about how register works and so is about linguistic ideas. Chapter 3 also provides an important introduction to the later description of the way in which pupils seem to develop awareness of different registers of language.

Again, if you wish to follow up your interest in relating these ideas to the types of writing recommended in *English for Ages 5 to 16* (DES 1989), you should read Chapter 4 which describes the register features of these different types of writing and the difficulties which they may present to pupils at each of the key stages.

Some readers will wish to know more about our findings (Littlefair 1988) of some pupils' awareness of the registers of varying types of writing. The research is based on genre ideas and is concerned with the awareness of some junior and secondary school readers of features of different types of writing. In Chapter 5 there is description of discussions which were held with pupils. The pupils were from 3rd-year junior school classes, 1st- and 4th-year secondary school classes and were either able, average or less able readers. The implication drawn from this inquiry is that we can only anticipate that some average and able readers who are coming towards the end of their compulsory education will understand how individual authors write for different purposes. In other words, these are the readers we can describe as competent readers of a range of types of writing.

Many teachers will be interested to study the continuum of development described in Chapter 6 which seems to be followed as pupils develop awareness of register. A pupil's position on the continuum will depend upon the type of writing which is being read. We have to estimate pupils' reading ability, therefore, over a range of types of writing.

An HMI report (1989: 10), *Reading Policy and Practice at Ages 5–14. Summer 1989* states that school policies for reading, 'were more informative and secure when dealing with aims and principles than with methodology'. In Chapter 7 there are suggestions for the practical application of a reading policy. These suggestions discuss aspects of reading for pleasure and information in the junior school, topic work in general and reading in the secondary school. There is description of *genre balance* and discussion of its value for discussion of pupils' reading at different stages of their school careers. There is a brief discussion of research which compares the genres of books read in the final 4th-year term of some junior school pupils and in their 1st secondary school term. The tables which compare the percentages of different genres of books read are recorded in Appendix 2.

The overall relevance for teachers of genre-based language teaching is discussed in Chapter 8 so that you may become aware of the position it advocates and some of the arguments which have been raised against that position. Genre-based language teaching in Australia has stimulated dynamic discussion. This chapter suggests that new ideas give new insights which extend our understanding of language education and which can be used in tune with well-proven methods.

This is not a book to be necessarily read from cover to cover but it is written so that you as the reader can decide your main purpose and follow your own reading plan.

Acknowledgements

This book is the result of several years study, thought and practical experience. My interest in language began whilst teaching in a comprehensive school where colleagues co-operated with me in implementing ideas of language across the curriculum.

For three years, I worked with Dr L. John Chapman at the Open University when we pursued the question of how far register is an important factor in learning to read. As a result of this work, I travelled to Australia to the Linguistics Department of Sydney University. From this base, I was able to visit schools, State education departments and teacher training institutions. I met academics, teachers and advisers who generously found time to discuss with me practical issues about language education. This experience confirmed my emergent sense of the importance of the new thinking about genre.

In England I have worked with both teachers and pupils. This co-operation enabled me to discuss with individual pupils their response to different registers of books. As a teacher, I am aware of how much reorganization this kind of work entails.

During all this time, I have been fortunate to have a family and friends who have borne my preoccupation with these matters with cheerful tolerance.

To all these people, I owe sincere thanks.

Alison B. Littlefair

CHAPTER 1

Different types of writing

Reading across the curriculum

Reading different types of writing is not, of course a new idea. The Bullock Report recommended, 'that by consultation all teachers should accept the responsibility for developing reading in their field and that certain shared principles should help them to fulfil it' (DES 1975 : 8.9). So language co-ordinators encouraged teachers across the curriculum to become aware of the problems faced by many pupils as they read the language of different subjects.

Many teachers in secondary school English departments were influenced by a research project undertaken at the London Institute of Education in the 1970s. In this project, pupils' own writing was studied and categorized into groups based on transactional, expressive and poetic functions of writing (Martin *et al.* 1976). Although the work was concerned with pupils' writing, it also provided a basis from which some schools began to discuss the different types of language used across the curriculum.

Much of the potential of this interest in the language demands of the curriculum was lost at the end of the 1970s mainly because no government money was found to fund well-informed language co-ordinators. The Kingman Report (DES 1988a) stimulated the debate about language in education. The later Cox Reports (DES 1988b; 1989) clearly demanded that teachers of English look at language variety. Meanwhile research in Australia has taken a new look at language education. It is this view which we will apply to categorizing the different types of writing listed in *English for Ages 5 to 16* (DES 1989).

Different types of writing in *English for Ages 5 to 16* (DES 1989)

Many types of writing are mentioned in the Programmes of Study for

Reading in *English for Ages 5 to 16* (DES 1989) which refer to pupils' reading in both primary and secondary school. The list is formidable and the range of writing is considerable:

stories, poetry, picture books, nursery rhymes,
folk tales, myths, legends, plays,
children's newspapers, guide-books,
labels, captions, notices, instructions, menus,
road-signs, logos, plans, maps, diagrams,
computer printouts,
dictionaries, word-books, fables,
'good non-fiction',
newspapers, magazines, catalogues,
lists of contents, indices, library classification list,
autobiographies, letters, diaries,
short stories, novels, the Bible,
literature from other countries,
pre-twentieth-century fiction,
travel books, consumer reports, text books,
contracts, information leaflets,
publicity material, advertisements,
leader columns, pressure group literature, brochures,
stage directions, manuals, forms, highway code,
thesauruses, atlases, encyclopediae, data bases.

In school, we usually classify books according to their subject. For example, in the primary school, books about number are probably together in a pile, or books concerned with a project may form a display. Teachers in a secondary school will be concerned with books related to their specialist subject. Clearly, this method is sensible because we use books as they are needed in various areas of the curriculum.

We could, however, take more of an overview of books. If you look at the very roughly organized list (above) of types of writing, you will see that we cannot really classify types according to subject. We have to look at this list rather differently.

Most readers will meet these different types of writing as they proceed through school. It is suggested that, 'as independence is strengthened, pupils should be encouraged to read more difficult texts and to look not only at what is said but at how meaning is expressed and how effects are achieved' (DES 1989: 16.11).

So, we are being urged to look at various types of writing in terms of their individual meanings. This seems a very involved task, but if we can differentiate and categorize these types according to the particular meanings they express, we will be in a position to plan our pupils' reading strategically. When authors set out to express their meaning, they have very definite purposes. We will find it very much easier to categorize the meanings of various types of writing if we look at the purposes of the writers.

Some different purposes for writing: the implication for genre

Here are four extracts taken from books read by some 1st-year secondary school pupils:

1. Victor appeared next morning just after breakfast. Dad was washing up and Mum was reading the paper when he looked round the door, carrying a string bag with a lettuce in it.
   'We're here,' said Victor. (Mark 1976)

2. The word *Dinosauria* (Die-no-sore-ee-a) means 'mighty or terrible lizards', and was given to this group early in the last century. About that time the first remains were being discovered, including some enormous bones. Since then any number of dinosaurs have been found all over the world, especially in America. (Leutscher 1971)

3. Addition
   Add these numbers together on the calculator.
   $397 + 268 + 105 =$
   Write down the answer.
   Now add the same numbers, but in this order.
   $268 + 397 + 105 =$
   Check the answer is the same as before. (*Using a Calculator, S.M.P. 11–16*)

4. **hotel** n. commercial establishment providing lodging and meals – hotel keeper, hotelier n. (*Collins Gem English Dictionary* 1985)

Clearly the authors of these extracts had quite different purposes in mind when they wrote these books:

The purpose of the author of Extract 1 is to write a story
The purpose of the author of Extract 2 is to write a description.
The purpose of the author of Extract 3 is to give instructions.
The purpose of the author of Extract 4 is to provide sequential definitions.

So, we could categorize different types of writing found in school on the basis of authors' purposes rather than on the subject areas. I want to suggest that authors who have similar purposes produce a particular *genre* of writing. For example, authors of detective stories have the purpose of writing a story which is about creating mystery and solving a crime.

Authors of science text books have the purpose of explaining natural phenomena to pupils of particular ages. These are different types or genres of writing because the authors' purposes are different.

Genres of books used in school

It was in order to have an overview of the different purposes of authors of books used in school that I surveyed over 100 books in use in some junior and secondary schools. I found that on the basis of authors' purposes for writing, we can categorize books in school into four major categories. There are, of course, many smaller categories or *sub-genres* within each major group.

Books in the literary genre

Authors who have a purpose of narrating, of describing personal or vicarious experience, or of experimenting with the use of language itself, write books which fall within the literary genre.

Some sub-genres mentioned in *English for Ages 5 to 16* (DES 1989) are: folk tales, short stories, poetry, plays, diaries.

Books in the expository genre

Authors who plan to describe or explain objectively, to inform, or discuss, or argue, will write books within the expository genre.

Some sub-genres mentioned in *English for Ages 5 to 16* (DES 1989) are: guide books, text books, newspapers, information leaflets, brochures.

Books in the procedural genre

Authors who wish to give instructions, or to initiate activities, will write books which fall within the procedural genre. These authors tell us how to undertake various learning strategies or how to complete tasks.

Some sub-genres mentioned in *English for Ages 5 to 16* (DES 1989) are: lists of instructions, guide books, stage directions, forms.

Books in the reference genre

Authors whose purpose is to write sequential information about particular topics, will write books which fall into the reference genre. These authors intend to provide information which can be reasonably easily referenced.

Some sub-genres mentioned in *English for Ages 5 to 16* (DES 1989) are: dictionaries, encyclopedias computer data, maps, catalogues.

Summary

So genres are the result of authors' purposes. Thus we can now describe:

Extract 1 as being within the literary genre.
Extract 2 as being within the expository genre.
Extract 3 as being within the procedural genre.
Extract 4 as being within the reference genre.

Similarly, we can categorize the types of writing listed in the programmes for study for reading in *English for Ages 5 to 16* (DES 1989) into literary, expository, procedural and reference genres as shown in Table 1.

We have used *genre* as the form of writing which authors choose in order to achieve their purposes. We should now understand that within genres, authors have to use the variety or *register* of language which they think is appropriate.

Genre and register are terms which we will look at a little more closely in Chapter 2.

Table 1 Categories (genres) of types of writing listed in the programme of study for reading in *English for Ages 5 to 16*

Literary genre

Programme of study for key stage 1 (ages 5–7)
stories, poetry, picture books, nursery rhymes, folk tales, myths, legends (16.22)
Programme of study for key stage 2 (ages 7–11)
stories, poems, drama, folk tales, fables (16.25)
Programme of study for key stages 3 and 4 (ages 11/12 to 14 and 14–16)
autobiographies, letters, diaries, short stories, novels, poetry, plays, literature from other countries (16.30)
Authorized version of the Bible, Wordsworth's poems, Dickens's novels, Shakespeare, pre-twentieth-century fiction (16.31)

Expository genre

Programmes of study for key stage 1 (ages 5–7)
children's newspapers, non-fiction/interest books (16.22)
information books (16.23)
Programmes for study for key stage 2 (ages 7–11)
good non-fiction, newspapers, magazines (16.25) advertisements (16.29)
Programme of study for key stages 3 and 4 (ages 11/12 to 14 and 14–16)
travel books, consumer reports, text books, contracts, information leaflets, publicity material, newspapers, magazines (16.34)
advertisements, leader columns, pressure group literature (16.40)

Procedural genre

Programme of study for key stage 1 (ages 5–7)
notices, books of instructions (16.22)
Programme of study for key stage 2 (ages 7–11)
Programme of study for key stages 3 and 4 (ages 11/12 to 14 and 14–16)
guide books, sets of instructions, manuals, stage directions, forms, highway code (16.34)

Reference genre

Programme of study for key stage 1 (ages 5–7)
plans, maps, diagrams, computer printouts (16.22)
dictionaries, word books, computer data, road signs, logos (16.23)
Programme of study for key stage 2 (ages 7–11)
lists of contents, indexes, library classification, library catalogues (16.28)
Programme of study for key stages 3 and 4 (ages 11/12 to 14 and 14–16)
dictionaries, thesauruses, atlases, encyclopediae (16.34)
subject reference books, adult encyclopedias, data bases (16.42)

CHAPTER 2

Genre and register

Genre

The term *genre* used to refer almost exclusively to different forms of literary writing. It has gradually widened its meaning so that it is now used to refer to other forms of writing besides those which are considered to be literary. In fact, *genre* is used commonly to refer to categories or groups of almost anything. I have noted references in the press to 'a genre of wine', 'the genre of the British Honours system', and even 'a genre of bikinis'!

In British schools, we have been aware of the importance of other forms of writing for some time. As we have seen, the research undertaken at the London Institute of Education in the 1970s alerted us to the implications of widening our perceptions of writing in education.

In America too, interest in a broad spectrum of writing activities was kindled by writers like Moffat and Hymes. Moffat (1968) wrote a highly influential book proposing that pupils should be made aware of all forms of language communication. He described correspondence, personal journal, autobiography, memoir, biography, chronicle, history, science and metaphysics. Hymes (1972) wrote about written genres such as poem, myth, tale, proverb, riddle, commercial form, letter and editorial. He saw that a major genre such as a church service includes different sub-genres: hymns, psalms and sermons.

Kinneavy *et al*. (1976: 7–8) describe their view of different forms of text which, in many ways, anticipates recent research about genres. They describe narrative as focusing 'on the dynamic aspects of reality', classification as not being 'concerned with the unique thing but with things as members of groups', and evaluation as being where 'the performance is measured up against a desired end and the value judgement is made in terms of the coincidence of performance and end'. They go on to describe forms of text as representing the way we view reality. Thus different text forms represent different ways of thinking and, as such, they have been debated since the time of the Ancient Greeks. We might think how traditional English literature teaching has maintained the dominance of narration, argument and exposition in pupils' written work in English.

We have already seen that authors have purposes which decide the particular form or genre they will use as they write. For example, the purpose of a novelist and the author of an instructional manual are quite different. The written form of their work is characteristic, for we can more or less predict some of the features of the genres they will write. For instance, we are very familiar with the form of a novel and of a newspaper. We would find it very strange if the two forms were mixed up. So we can see that purpose and genre are closely linked and further that we will help our developing readers if we point this out to them.

Genre is seen as having a further purpose: that of social relevance. We have to ask ourselves why particular genres have the form they do. Why do we write reports or persuasive arguments in certain ways? The answer must be that the genre forms have developed these meanings over centuries within our culture. As we learn to use the genre forms, we continue the ways of expressing meaning in our culture. Martin *et al.* (n.d.: 59) give a down-to-earth definition of genres, 'Genres represent the most efficient ways cultures have at a given point in time of going about their business.' Thus, if we are to take part fully in our society, we should have experience of a wide range of genres.

At the beginning of the 1980s an important language development project began in Sydney where a group of linguists and teachers began to look at the types of writing produced by primary school children. As they considered the types of writing, the researchers began to categorize them into genres and to look at the developmental pattern of the children's writing which they reviewed (Martin and Rothery 1981). As this research developed, the linguists, led by Jim Martin, a former student of Halliday, began to describe the genres themselves.

The linguists were interested in the relationship between the genre form and the the language used by the writer within that form. A genre has no independent meaning. That meaning is expressed through language but the language itself is not entirely the writer's free choice. Writers use language which is appropriate to their purposes and therefore to the form of genre they have chosen. Thus writers will use a particular variety of language which they think is appropriate. Such language variety is the *register* of language.

Register

Systemic linguists see register as an abstract linguistic concept. It is the way in which writers and speakers express themselves. Essentially, register refers to the way in which language varies according to the situation in which it is spoken or written. Register is the means by which a situation is analysed so that it can be expressed through language. This means that register reflects what is being spoken or written about, who is being spoken or written to and how the message is given. These three aspects of a situation are termed by linguists *field*, *mode* and *tenor*.

The field (what is spoken or written about), the mode (how language is used) and tenor (the attitude of the speaker or writer to the listener or reader, and to the subject) are expressed through language, that is through the speaker's or listener's choice of vocabulary and grammar. We can now look at the register of the extracts from different genres which we have already discussed.

Examples of registers of different genres of books read by some 1st-year secondary school pupils

Example of register: literary genre (story)

Victor appeared next morning just after breakfast, Dad was washing up and Mum was reading the paper when he looked round the door, carrying a string bag with a lettuce in it.
    'We're here,' said Victor. (Mark 1976)

Field: adventure story.
Mode: written to give dynamic story line, events happening in sequence ('next morning', 'just after', 'when').
Tenor: written to interest readers in top juniors or lower secondary school classes; informal writing, conversation.

Example of register: expository genre (information)

The word *Dinosauria* (Die-no-sore-ee-a) means 'mighty or terrible lizards', and was given to this group early in the last century. About that time the first remains were being discovered, including some enormous bones. Since then any number of dinosaurs have been found all over the world, especially in America. (Leutscher 1971)

Field: description of dinosaurs.
Mode: language of science, more complex, technical words, sense of a sequence of events ('in the last century', 'about that time', 'since

then') although these phrases describing time are more complex than those used in the last extract.

Tenor: written for young readers who want information; writing is distanced from the reader and therefore formal.

Example of register: procedural genre (instructions)

Addition
Add these numbers together on the calculator.
397 + 268 + 105 =
Write down the answer.
Now add the same numbers, but in this order.
268 + 397 + 105 =
Check the answer is the same as before. (*'Using a Calculator'*, *S.M.P. 11–16*)

Field: instructions for working on a calculator.
Mode: format is a list, no joining of sentences, numbers and mathematical signs.
Tenor: written for pupils who are commencing work with calculators; sentences are commands and therefore formal.

Example of register: reference genre (dictionary)

hotel n. commercial establishment providing lodging and meals – hotel keeper, hotelier n. (*Collins Gem English Dictionary* 1985)

Field: definition of a word.
Mode: format is one item from a list, no sentences and no joining of ideas, use of abbreviation, use of technical sign ('n').
Tenor: written for readers who are beginning to use dictionaries; simplified explanations but remains formal.

Summary

Genre has come to mean:

> *a class or category of things*
> *it relates closely to the author's or speaker's purpose*
> *it has social significance because a particular genre form has evolved as a way of organizing meaning within a culture*

Register reflects:

> *what we are speaking or writing about (field)*
> *how we use language (mode)*
> *who we are speaking or writing to and our attitude to the subject (tenor)*

Authors make choices of vocabulary, grammar and non-verbal features such as type and illustrations. These choices are not made in an *ad hoc* manner because authors are constrained by how they can best express meaning within the genre they have chosen. The way in which register actually works is discussed in Chapter 3. There is a more detailed description of the concepts of genre and register in the Technical Appendix.

How does register work?

We have already seen that register comes about because of the interaction of the field, mode and tenor of a social situation. In this sense, register is an abstract concept which teachers may feel is the province of linguists. However, if we study register closely and use the knowledge to inform our teaching, we will be in a far better position to help pupils to write for different purposes and to read books which are written for different purposes.

So register results from our situation as a speaker or writer. We have also seen that it is expressed mainly through the choices we make from vocabulary and grammar in order to express what we wish to communicate, how we communicate, and with whom we communicate. Again, there is interaction between these aspects. Thus, if I lecture to people I have never met before and who wish to understand something about the register of language, my register will be different from the register I would use if I were to lecture to colleagues who have studied the subject for many years, because I will be familiar with the latter group and will be aware of their greater prior knowledge of the subject.

We implicitly make choices of vocabulary and grammatical constructions as we speak or write. When we read, we engage with text which has a register which has been chosen by the author. As fluent readers, we engage with varied registers competently.

If, however, we are to help the majority of young readers become familiar with a range of registers, then we must become far more explicitly aware of how register works. This means that we should study in greater detail how the field, the mode and the tenor are expressed through language so that we will be able to provide many examples and experiences of different language use for our pupils.

Field: how does the language indicate what is being talked or written about?

Field is concerned with the content of a communication. The content might be about objective features or about the writer's own thoughts and feelings. The field is made clear mainly by the author's choice of vocabulary.

When children begin to learn to read, we usually make sure that the words they meet are those with which they are probably already familiar. The vocabulary of early reading is often very similar to the vocabulary of speech. However, as children begin to read more advanced stories and, certainly as they begin to read other genres of books, they meet less familiar vocabulary. As teachers, we have to be aware of when less familiar vocabulary is experienced by readers and be prepared to help them overcome possible difficulties.

The vocabulary of text books is likely to be *field specialist*, that is vocabulary which is particular to a subject as in this extract from a history of early Cambridge:

> Ancient documents show that the settlement was occupied by many other armies including Britons, Romans, Danes and Normans. Two important Roman roads crossed Cambridge. One was the route from Colchester to Chester, on the border of Wales and is called Via Devana. (Graham-Cameron 1977)

Clearly, as pupils begin to learn subject specializations, they will meet texts which will contain a greater number of technical words. Sometimes these words are explained by the writer and sometimes the writer assumes that the technical vocabulary is understood. The more technical the subject is, then the more technical the content words become and understanding is difficult.

In some texts, vocabulary may change its meaning according to subject. A *crust* will mean one thing in a cookery recipe and another thing in a geography text where it appears as the *earth's crust*. Where words have different spellings for different meanings, there may be problems of understanding. For instance, *plane* in mathematics has a different meaning from *plain* in geography. Some pupils may not recognize the changed spelling and their understanding may be hindered.

Obviously, there is close association between the vocabulary and the content of a book. As soon as authors decide on a subject, they use words which are associated with that subject. One way of introducing pupils to topic work is to ask them to *brainstorm* ideas by suggesting words which they associate with that particular subject. So brainstorming the topic of the Ancient Egyptians might result in a list of content words which would begin as follows: *pyramids*, *pharoah*, *slaves*, *tomb*, *Valley of the Kings*, *temple*, *Nile*, *gods*, *funeral*, *gold*, *blocks of stone*, *papyrus*, *scribes*.

The children are, in fact, establishing the field but this is just one aspect of undertaking a topic which has to be considered by teacher and pupils. There remain the questions of how the project is to be produced, what form it will take, what kind of language is to be used and who it is being produced for. These questions have to be resolved before an appropriate register can be produced.

It is not necessary to be an expert to recognize that some words in our vocabulary are used more frequently than others. Children may not understand the content of a book if the words are unusual but we should understand that this problem may be only part of the difficulty of a text. The Bullock Report (DES 1975) warned of the breadth of difficulties facing children as they begin to study subject specializations in the secondary schools, ' . . . but the most obvious demand that for a wider and more specialized vocabulary, is not the principal difficulty' (12.3). Thus there is good reason for us to look in some detail at the way in which other aspects of register work.

Mode: how is the language expressed?

Mode is mainly concerned with how the text is constructed and which medium of communication is used. For instance, in reading, we are looking at written language which might be in a book or on a work-sheet or on a blackboard etc.

We use vocabulary and grammar to express the mode of a written text. Some linguists refer to the *language patterning* which we use. By this, they mean that certain kinds of language pattern are created as grammar and vocabulary interact. If you look at the four extracts we studied in Chapters 1 and 2, you will perhaps agree that we could describe each extract as having a different overall pattern of language from the other.

Horrowitz (1985) has suggested that five types of text patterns can be found in school texts. The temporal pattern or sequence of events is usually found in story books. Of course, some writers manipulate events as in flashbacks or in views of the future. Sometimes, writers of history texts use a sequential pattern to describe past events.

A different pattern is used by most writers of scientific text books where they are usually concerned with cause and effect and problem and solution as in this sentence from a health book used by 3rd-year junior readers: 'Pain receptors are clustered thickly on the surface of the eye, which is why dirt in the eye is so painful' (Ward 1982). This pattern is about cause and effect and not about a sequence of events just as the following extract has a pattern of problem and solution: 'Until about 1750 windmills had to be turned round by hand to face the wind. Then the fan tail was developed' (Wright 1976a).

Different text patterns may overlap each other in the same book. For instance, a science text may contain both a cause and effect pattern and a problem and solution pattern. Horrowitz suggests that problem and solution patterns are principally found in writing which is concerned with economics, social studies, geography and psychology.

Other patterns are the 'compare and contrast' patterns of science as in this extract: 'Although Copernicus and Kepler discovered much about how the planets moved around the Sun, they did not understand what kept them in orbit and why they did not fall into the Sun' (Brown 1984). Horrowitz suggests this is the major pattern of mathematics, social studies, history and foreign language learning. In addition, there are many books such as dictionaries and encyclopediae, which are mainly in the form of lists.

Again it is important that teachers of reading should be aware of types of text patterning for they represent ways in which writers organize meaning. We should be able to help developing readers understand the meaning of texts by looking at how the purposes of writers are expressed through language. These different overall patterns of written texts are made possible because of the various devices which writers use to make their text coherent.

Ways of linking within a text

We are coherent as writers and speakers because of the links of meaning within our conversation or writing. If you look at Part 1 of the model of language in the Kingman Report (DES 1988a), you will see that it is headed 'The forms of the English language'. In fact, this section is largely concerned with the way in which we link meaning within our speech and as we read books. One of the most significant ways in which writers link different aspects of their texts is by using *cohesive devices*.

L.J. Chapman (1983:44) refers to cohesion as a mechanism which binds 'text together into a whole meaningful unit'. Cohesive ties relate one element in a text with another and in so doing they provide links for readers as they follow continuous written text.

Reference ties are introduced at one particular point in the text and closed at another point in the text. Chapman (1987) suggests that as soon as readers meet the first part of a cohesive tie, they anticipate the second part of the tie. For instance, when we read, 'Peter kicked the ball and then he chased after it', we know that *he* refers to *Peter* and *it* to *ball*. If we did not understand these relationships, then we would have great difficulty in understanding the text.

As pupils read information books, some may have difficulty following the meaning. This extract from a book for 3rd-year junior school readers may well be misunderstood, 'The mummy was dragged on a decorated sledge up a long causeway to the Burial Temple. After a service to the gods, it was finally placed in the pyramid' (Unstead 1959). Will some readers assume that both sledge and mummy were left in the pyramid or that the mummy is removed from the sledge?

As readers cope with more sophisticated pieces of written work, the complexities of cohesion will increase and we may have to point out the subtleties of the links of meaning. For instance, 'Throughout his evolution, first crouched timidly in the dark, then huddled by a fire clutching a stone or club, man has been at the mercy of a determined predator' (McSweeney and Debes 1975). This is an extract included in an anthology for more senior readers. Are we sure that all 4th-year secondary school readers, will understand that *his* links with the later *man*? Certainly Chapman's research (1987) suggests that we should not be complacent about such comprehension by older pupils.

Conjunctions are most important cohesive devices. Often teachers have difficulty in persuading young writers that there are other conjunctions besides the ubiquitous *and*. Some conjunctions indicate that things are being classified such as *for example*; others indicate that one thing is being contrasted with another: *in other words*. Some conjunctions indicate that things are being varied: *but, however*. Other conjunctions refer to time, manner, cause: *then, afterwards, at once, similarly*. If you refer back to the extracts from books used as examples of genre and register in Chapters 1 and 2, you will note the significant use of *which, if, then, although*.

There is research (Binkley 1983) that suggests that writers within different subject areas use characteristic cohesive devices. Conjunctions may indicate the author's way of thinking. Even in a simple expository text, pupils can be alerted that use of *however* indicates a change of idea or opinion as in:

> This is a cheaper and more efficient way of making large amounts of bread. However, many people prefer to smell freshly-baked bread in their local bakery than to pick up a loaf from a supermarket shelf. (Turner 1988)

Conjunctions such as *so that, so, since*, enable the writer to state a cause and to express the effect. This may be an unusual language pattern, but is one which teachers can point out as they help readers to understand the meaning of the text.

You may not have considered that vocabulary itself provides cohesion within a text. Words may have links. Synonyms are words which have the same meaning, such as *valour* and *courage*. Antonyms are words which have opposite meanings, such as *open* and *closed*. Hyponyms are words which can be considered to be part of a single class of meaning, such as *rose, primrose, anemone*, which are hyponyms of *flower*. All give cohesion to a text because they reiterate a common meaning. Cohesion is also affected when words are repeated in a text and when there are words which frequently occur together as in the phrase, *bread and butter*.

Cohesion works along with register in creating what Halliday (1985) calls *the texture of text*. It is perhaps not surprising then that cohesion and register have been found to be important factors in reading development (Chapman 1987).

Ways of expressing meaning

Writers therefore use cohesion to produce a coherent piece of work. They also use a variety of grammar and vocabulary features as they express their meaning.

Abstract language When pupils enter the secondary school, they usually meet more formal writing than they have previously experienced. If we are to understand the kind of difficulty which many of these pupils face as they try to read more formal writing, we have to look at the way in which it is organized.

When children have a conversation, they use language which is straightforward. The same straightforward language is used in children's early stories. In other words, things are referred to as nouns, actions are verbs, describing is achieved by using adjectives and adverbs, and joining is done by conjunctions (Wignell 1987: 16). Halliday (1985) calls this straightforward language *congruent*.

By contrast, writers of text books use language which is more abstract and which Halliday calls *grammatical metaphor*.

The following sentence is expressed in congruent language: 'The journalist drove to town quickly and looked for a parking space.' Compare the formality of this version of the same statement: 'After driving with speed to town, a parking space was sought by the journalist.'

Halliday (1984: 24) uses this example of two versions of an instruction: 'Credit cards have been specially coded and will be issued only when credit has been checked in the normal way.' It is more likely that this kind of instruction will be expressed as follows: 'Issue of the specially coded credit cards will be subject to normal credit checking procedures.'

This is abstract language. People do not feature very much in this language which refers mainly to ideas. In fact, adult conversation often contains examples of this kind of language. If young readers do not begin to become familiar with this form of language, they will have difficulty in coping with the written language of the secondary school and with many of the ways in which language is used in adult life.

Complex introductions   A feature of this more abstract language is the complex opening of sentences. Consider this sentence: 'From the craggy summit could be seen the dusty road stretching from the fertile banks of the Nile to the Valley of the Kings.' There is an involved introduction to the sentence. Readers have to assume who is on the summit of the hill for the subject is not stated. In addition, readers may not fully appreciate what is meant by *stretching* or who or what is stretching and where it is stretching to. Such may be the problems in comprehension for pupils as they meet more complex registers.

Of course, there is no suggestion that we should return to any explicit teaching of clause analysis. There is, however, suggestion that, by becoming increasingly aware of these complexities, we will be in a better position to help readers at all stages of development. If we are aware of abstract language, we can seize the opportunity to read this kind of language to young pupils and to encourage them to read it for themselves. It is through increased familiarity with this mode of expression, that our pupils will become more prepared to unravel the mysteries of the meaning of more formal texts.

Vocabulary   Words may have content meaning or they may have purely grammatical meaning. If you look at the following sentence, the content words are printed normally, whilst the grammatical words are emphasized: 'Andrew noticed several rolls *of* carpet stacked *against the* back door (Mark 1976).

When we speak, we use many grammatical words but when we write we use far more content words. Ure (1969) explains that grammatical words have to do with action whereas a majority of content words has to do with reflection. In expository writing, the content words may be technical which will increase the problem of understanding.

The sentence, 'Issue of the specially coded credit cards will be subject to normal credit checking procedures,' is an excellent example of dense vocabulary. You might identify the content words: *issue, specially coded, credit, cards, subject, normal, checking, procedures*. The number of content words here packs tightly the meaning of the instruction and we have to read it carefully in order to understand its message.

Once we become aware of how some authors pack meaning into sentences, we are far more aware of the difficulties pupils may face as they read information books and endeavour to gather information from them.

Look at this extract from an encyclopedia used with top junior pupils:

'LOCUST . . . A migrating swarm of locusts is so huge and dense that it darkens the sky, and when the insects alight to feed they devour every green plant and blade of grass within sight' (*Children's Britannica 1964*). You may decide that the vocabulary will be reasonably familiar to your pupils, but you should also consider how much information is being given in the explanations. Readers, and particularly young researchers, have to 'unpack' the meaning and this may not be an easy task.

Opening and closing Different genres may have particular kinds of introduction or preface which give clues to authors' purposes so it is useful to discuss these features.

Most importantly, the writers of many expository texts will include methods for information retrieval. These features appear at the opening and closing of the information books. This is the feature which is perhaps noticed most by teachers. In the same way that we encourage children to use the index, list of contents or glossary to help them gather information, so we should note how other features of the register can help understanding.

Non-verbal features

We should remember that presentation is a feature of register, for writers use many methods in order to enhance the meaning of their texts. Various kinds of type may be used at times for emphasis. Are we sure that all our pupils understand the inference of the print? It may be that differences in the type used to print the page may cause problems to less able readers (Tinker 1963).

We have to be sure that our readers really do understand what the writer is signalling. For example, we may overlook that some readers may need to be told exactly what instruction is being given, as on this page from a science book used with 1st-year secondary school pupils, '1 Write the heading *Find the freezing temperature of acetophenone* in your book' (Fielding 1984).

Are we sure that all our pupils take in their stride two columns of print on some pages of expository text instead of the one column of print found in most story books? Are we sure that all our pupils have understood the relationship of illustrations to the meaning of the text? In some cases, the meaning of a page of text may be largely dependent upon illustrations, diagrams, graphs etc. Illustrations and pictures of all kinds may be used by authors as aids to comprehension. The way in which illustrations are arranged on a page can act as a cohesive device. Again, pupils can be encouraged to read captions. However, there must be clear relationship between the written text and the illustrations. Unfortunately, this is not always the case. Most teachers will be familiar with books where the illustrations are not related to the text or where diagrams are not fully explained.

Different types of writing can be presented on a page in so many ways. In schools, the number of pupils with access to using desk-top publishing is steadily increasing. Wray and Medwell (1989) have discussed the implications of desk-top publishing for pupils' development of literacy. As pupils become more aware of the link between meaning and ways of presentation, they may well become far more aware of the ways in which different types of writing which they read are presented. This is one way in which modern technology gives us the tools to help us make pupils far more aware of aspects of writing which previously we may have overlooked.

Tenor: who is the language written for?

Tenor is concerned with the relationship between the speaker or writer and the listener or reader. It is also concerned with the speaker's or writer's attitude and feelings to the subject. Professional writers judge their readers and choose a tenor which they feel is appropriate. Of course, we might not always agree with their judgement. We may read or write a text which is very formal in that there is little relationship intended between the writer and reader. Such a formal tenor is often used by the expert who is writing for literate, well-informed readers. At the other extreme, the writer of a narrative for young readers will write in a very familiar tenor.

Here is great implication for the types of writing which we read in school. Sometimes authors try to create some kind of rapport with their young readers but sometimes they do not succeed and pupils then read books in which the language appears to be unreal and remote. It may even be that some authors of books to be used in school write for the teachers who will buy the books and not for the pupils.

How are different tenors expressed?

We are able to use a choice of moods as we speak or write. Thus 'Shut the door!' may well be a sharp command but if this were a spoken command, then intonation would be used in addition to indicate the tenor. Written commands are quite common in books in the procedural genre as in a mathematics or science textbook. Usually the tenor is fairly formal as in the instruction: 'Check your apparatus'.

Sometimes writers use auxiliary or helping verbs along with the main verbs. These are named *modal* verbs and they suggest uncertainty, definiteness, vagueness, possibility. Examples of these helping verbs are:

can, might, should. The use of these modal verbs become very important particularly when we encourage readers to look at persuasive writing of all kinds for these verbs tell us a great deal about writers' attitudes.

Different tenors can be achieved by the use of the active and passive voice. Writers of narrative for young readers usually write in the active voice where the subject of an action in a sentence is clear. Thus in, 'The boy hid in the old shed' it is clear who is hiding. However, if we read, 'The book was taken from the library' we are not clear who has actually taken the book. Use of the passive voice is very common as texts become more formal. The writer is distanced from the action and it is far more difficult to feel involved as a reader. Writers of science text books use the passive voice frequently. Probably this is because science is an objective study and not one where personal feelings have importance. Thus the following sentence is typical of this use of the passive voice in science text books: 'The effect of this chemical reaction is seen clearly as the test-tube is held to the light.'

Whether the tenor is formal or not depends largely on whether the first, second or third person is used. If the third person (*they* is often understood) is used then the writing is reasonably formal as in these sentences from *Swallows and Amazons* (Ransome 1930): 'Directly over the stern on the far side of the lake there was a white cottage. On the hillside above the cottage was a group of tall pines.'

If the writer uses the second person (*you*), then there is definite recognition of the listener or reader and the tenor may be fairly informal as in this extract from a history book for 9–13 year-olds:

> When you last read about historical characters such as Julius Caesar, Francis Drake or Napoleon, did you ever stop to think that your ancestors were alive at the same time? (Burrell 1988)

If the first person singular (*I*) is used, then as readers we are aware of the author as the person and we may feel more involved in the text. This becomes far more personal if the plural (*we*) is used as in some information books where the author wishes to establish a rapport with young readers. We should be aware that information books written in this way may engage the interest of young readers but those young readers are not really being prepared for the register of more sophisticated information books. Consider this sentence in an information book about a wild life park and see whether you agree with my last statement:

> Soon I reached the wild life park. I paid at the entrance and bought a guide book. Then I drove in. I spent the day meeting some of the people who worked with the animals. (Pluckrose 1988)

My rationale for using a fairly informal tenor in this book is that I anticipate that my readers are already able to read a range of genres and I wish to explain a rather complex subject in reader-friendly terms!

Summary

We have looked at some of the different linguistic and non-linguistic features of field, mode and tenor aspects of register. It is important to understand now that no one feature can really be considered in isolation when considering a register. The factors are interactive; each has an influence on register. Nor is there a formula which determines the register which should appear in particular genres. There are likely choices which authors will make as they write certain genres but as their purposes for writing change so will their choice of vocabulary and grammar.

It is important that we are able to estimate the level of difficulty of the registers which are used by writers. If we are able to do this in an informed way, we will be far more aware of the complexities of the reading tasks facing pupils at different stages of their development as competent readers.

CHAPTER 4

Reading different types of writing

We should now look at how we can use knowledge of the main linguistic features of register within the classroom. In Chapter 1 a list is given of the types of writing listed in the programmes of study for reading in *English for Ages 5 to 16* (DES 1989). The different types of writing are listed under four major categories of genres of books.

Reading different types of literary writing

Key stage 1 (ages 5–7)
(stories, poetry, picture books, nursery rhymes, folk tales, myths, legends)

At this stage, most pupils are beginning to read. They are usually introduced to reading through story which they listen to as well as read. Stories are concerned with imagination and often fantasy which are such important elements in children's emotional, affective and creative development. Children become implicitly aware of the characteristic language of stories. Even the arrangement of a story with a main title and then chapter headings, which may simply be the number of the chapter itself, becomes familiar. Young readers soon learn to anticipate that a fairy story is likely to follow the opening phrase, 'Once upon a time'. Picture books help very young readers to gain familiarity with a pattern of events which occur in a sequence. As readers develop, they expect a story to contain a succession of events which will be interesting and probably adventurous.

Rothery (1980) discusses a common narrative structure which is characterized by setting, a complication and a resolution. Once pupils are aware of this kind of structure, they can be encouraged to make inferences and to predict outcomes of the story. Katherine Perera (1984) describes fiction as being about people, as having many personal pronouns, subjects which are usually the subject of the action, chronological patterns of organization, easy joining ways of making connections and relatively few nouns.

Here is an example of a simple way in which writers for young children use joining devices: 'A little while later, the young man came out of the house. Mrs Better came to the door with him, and handed him some money' (McCullagh 1985). *And* is easily seen as a joining word, but we should ensure that our young readers really do know that 'him', which appears twice, refers to the young man and not to another character who has just been mentioned. In this book there are illustrations which help comprehension but their importance for understanding may have to be pointed out to some readers. The story also contains conversation. Most young readers will become quite used to the punctuation of conversation. These written conversations are of course the language of speech which readers can usually understand. In general, readers' understanding is helped by the dynamics of stories.

Nursery rhymes provide experience of the cadence of words, of rhyme, of different arrangement of written language, of fun with words. This kind of experience with another way of arranging language continues as poetry is introduced. Poetry is a language form which has all manners of idiosyncracies. At this key stage, children just enjoy the jingles and the rhyme as in,

> I think mice
> Are rather nice.

> (Fyleman 1956)

We should recognize that the introduction of folk tales, myths and legends indicates that pupils will read yet another sub-genre in the literary genre.

Key stage 2 (ages 7–11)
(Stories, poems, drama, folk tales, fables)

Readers will begin to read more sophisticated stories where they will meet 'flashbacks' and more complex complications within the story itself. Sometimes, the content of a story may be more sophisticated although the register itself may be fairly simple as in:

> An astronaut was lying on the rock on the edge of a wide dark hole. Arun got to him, and pulled him clear. It was Fred.
>   'Switch over to a new air cylinder,' called Dr Hawk, coming up.
> (McCullagh 1970)

Enid Blyton produced an amazing number of plots which young readers love and many adults still remember reading her books with great enjoyment. She wrote in a fairly simple mode and, whilst not wishing to inhibit the fun of reading, we may have to help some readers to become familiar with more complex registers as in the following extract:

> And now, very calmly, with that curious wisdom that seems to come so often to small children in times of hardship, he began to make changes here and there in some of the things that he did, so as to save his strength (Dahl 1964).

Roald Dahl uses complex expressions, for you will have seen that this is a very long sentence with an involved introduction. However, here is a much-loved story which provides opportunity for pupils to hear and read complex language.

In the following sentence, the action of the sentence is delayed until the end: 'While the dogs searched and the Nannies cried on each other's shoulders, Mrs Dearly telephoned Mr Dearly' (Smith 1957). Readers have to assimilate the introduction until they come eventually to the main point of the sentence. Some readers may need a little help to understand the way the author is writing. This kind of expression is quite a jump from the clear information given by McCullagh above and we should be aware of the problem of understanding which some readers may experience.

In the same book, readers meet figurative language as in ' . . . he lay staring at the fire, chewing the wicker of his basket *as a man might have smoked a pipe.*' Again, we cannot assume that metaphors and similes are understood by the majority of our readers. Certainly, as pupils come to read more complicated plots, they meet more formal expression. For all the familiarity of the story form, we cannot assume that readers will automatically manage to read a range of registers within that genre.

Understanding of more sophisticated writing may also depend upon general knowledge on the part of the reader. Dahl's *The Grand High Witch* is about a grandmother obeying the instructions of a will. We must be sure that our readers have at least some background knowledge which will allow them to construct the meaning of the content area itself, for different readers may reconstruct varying meaning from the same text.

Key stages 3 and 4 (ages 11/12 to 14 and 14–16)
(autobiographies, letters, diaries, short stories, novels,
poetry, plays, literature from other countries, Authorized
version of the Bible, Wordsworth's poems, Dickens's
novels, Shakespeare, pre-twentieth-century fiction)

As readers meet longer novels, they will meet further formality of language. Adams commences *Watership Down* with a long description which begins:

> The primroses were over. Towards the edge of the wood, where the ground became open and sloped down to an old fence and a brambly ditch beyond, only a few fading patches of pale yellow still showed among the dog's mercury and oak-tree roots.

There is no sense of action here but a long description and some readers may discard the book at first glance. There is no suggestion that lessons about language structure be given but the linguistically informed teacher is in a position to explain something about the way Adams creates an effect. This kind of teaching has previously occurred where older pupils have studied literature. These readers have become familiar with literary devices. They learn to understand the implication of writing such as,

> But his mind staggered before the extent of his ambitions. . . . The poison drained back into its proper glands: he was admired, no one insulted him. . . . (Greene 1938)

The proposals for the National Curriculum in English advocates the introduction of Wordsworth's poems, Dickens's novels, Shakespeare, the Authorized version of the Bible into the reading of all pupils. We have to encourage pupils to become involved reading more sophisticated types of writing. Margaret Meek (1988) points out that in this way, there is more likelihood that readers will themselves become familiar with different registers and their reading will become more flexible. Our better readers will cope with this kind of language but so may our more reluctant readers if we note the possible problems which may inhibit their understanding, and take some time to talk about different ways of expression.

Letters, diaries and autobiographies are termed 'literary non-fiction' in Level 7 for Reading Attainment in *English for Ages 5 to 16* (DES 1989). That description is apt, but within the categories of major genres these types of writing are placed firmly in the literary genre. The reason for this is that the authors' writing purposes are to express their own experience. We may have to teach the language form of diaries and personal letters and point out features, such as how these writers often use abbreviated language as in the *Journals of Dorothy Wordsworth* (Moorman 1971).

> Wednesday, 21 May, 1800. Went often to spread the linen which was bleaching – a rainy day and a very wet night.

In this way, we can encourage readers to understand that different forms of writing are appropriate to the purpose of the author.

Reading different types of expository writing

The purposes of authors who write books in the expository genre are to explain, describe, argue. Katherine Perera (1984) describes this type of writing as being about processes, objects and abstract concepts. Broadly speaking, it is the way in which subject areas are written and often spoken about and therefore it is the language of text books, particularly in the secondary school. Later in life, our pupils will meet it as the language of government, of law, of banking, of professional concern and thus we can ill afford to ignore it.

Key stage 1 (ages 5–7)
(children's newspapers, non-fiction/interest books,
information books)

The programme of study in *English for Ages 5 to 16* (DES 1989) recommends that young pupils be introduced to non-fiction in general and to information books in particular. This is sound planning, for if young readers are to become flexible then they should become familiar with more formal genres of writing and their registers.

However, there are all kinds of problems concerning the selection of expository books for these young readers. Publishers have responded swiftly to the increasing awareness that pupils should become familiar with information books from an early age and thus there is an increasing number of expository books available for younger readers. We have already noticed that some authors use registers which may not be appropriate if pupils are to develop a familiarity with the characteristic registers of non-fiction writing.

We must be very clear as to why we ask young pupils to read non-fiction. Some non-fiction books are sometimes extremely attractive but inappropriate for study purposes. Sometimes writers of information books for younger pupils concentrate only on the field or subject area of the books. Probably the purpose of these writers is to provide interesting books about a particular subject. These books are not really appropriate for children who are asked to read the book in order to extract information. For example, a book may contain some descriptive writing. This register suddenly changes into that of a story by the introduction of conversation. Indeed, it seems quite common for creatures in junior information books to suddenly break into conversation:

> 'This is my tree,' said the bee.
> 'This is my tree,' said the ladybird. (Cutting and Cutting 1989)

Description is sometimes written as a conversation which is rather a contradiction of expository writing:

> The little seedlings are beginning to grow. Soon they will have more leaves.
> (Ginn Science 1988)

Teachers who have knowledge of register, will be able to choose books which are appropriate for the reading purposes of their pupils.

Of course, we want to introduce children to non-fiction topics in as interesting a way as possible. However, we have also to introduce children to the way in which non-fiction topics are usually written about. In fact, it is difficult to separate topic and language expression as readers meet more sophisticated writing.

Key stage 2 (ages 7–11)
('good non-fiction', newspapers, magazines, advertisements)

At this stage, it is suggested in *English for Ages 5 to 16* (DES 1989: 16.26) that pupils should 'hear good non-fiction read aloud'. I have already referred to inappropriate writing of non-fiction. We should consider the main linguistic characteristics which readers at this stage will begin to experience in good non-fiction.

Expository writing is characterized by registers unlike those used by writers of books in the literary genre. At first glance, these registers are certainly not so engaging to read because the dynamics of the texts are so different.

When children read fiction, they become involved in the action of the plot. Children watch similar action in films. It is very much more difficult to become interested in texts which do not have a chronological structure. Perera (1986: 56) lists the types of text organization into chronological and non-chronological categories:

chronological: children's fiction, biographical accounts, instructions, accounts of processes
non-chronological: descriptions of people, descriptions of objects, statements of principles, hypotheses

A good deal of the writing in the expository genre is non-chronological and is structured by linguistic features that we discussed in Chapter 3. Our readers will be helped if we assist them to anticipate these features and the reasons why writers use them.

On the whole, authors of more formal types of writing select a tenor which distances them from their reader. Often this sense of distance is achieved by use of the passive voice and by writing in the third person. It is important that pupils be given opportunities to listen to, to read and to write in this way.

The following sentence comes from a history book for junior school readers: 'Ploughing was one of the main activities in autumn and winter' (Triggs 1979). In this extract, there is no mention of who is ploughing. Do our readers know? This kind of expression is a large jump from our readers' experience of the way stories are written. Some readers may have difficulty in understanding that the Saxons are the subject of the sentence.

It is recommended that readers at key stage 2 are introduced to newspapers. Of course, there is a wide range of writing in the newspaper world and we can use different newspapers to illustrate different ways of expressing meaning. We might, for example, note the way in which journalists may write about local or national news:

> Four police forces have been alerted. . . . (*Cambridge Evening News* 13 October 1989)

> Initial inquiries by Avon and Somerset Police were made last year. (*Guardian* 18 October 1989)

Here we can illustrate use of the passive voice as the grammar which the journalists have chosen to report news. We can show that by making this choice, they have achieved a sense of objectivity. We can also point out that information is usually written about in the same way.

We have already looked in Chapter 3 at the use of complex openings to sentences as a possible aspect of the mode. This aspect certainly appears in many expository texts. In the junior school, however, pupils may read information books which are written more simply. In this history book for juniors, the author mainly chooses simple introductions to sentences as in this sentence, '*The females* are sharing out the fruit, roots and nuts they collected yesterday' (Burrell 1988).

In contrast, we might notice that some information books read by junior school readers are written more formally:

> Little more than two metres long, Amazon river dolphins are very brightly coloured compared with most other members of the dolphin family. The older they are the pinker they become.
> In some parts of the Amazon Basin, where they live, they even help the local people. They come to the call of the fishermen, leading fish from deeper water to their nets in the shallows. (Carwardine 1987)

Information often comes at the end of complex sentences. This may result in the reader missing the new information. In the last extract, pupils may not understand that the personal reference tie *they* in the second paragraph refers to dolphins which are mentioned at the very beginning of the previous paragraph.

As we have seen, junior school pupils may read simplified history texts. Whilst these books may well create great interest which is so important, it should be remembered that formal history texts are not usually written as narrative. On the other hand, some history books are very attractively produced but the teacher must be aware that the text may contain a formal register of language.

We may consider some junior school history books to be old-fashioned but we should assess just how far such books are in fact helping pupils to become more aware of the register features of expository writing. The following description of the pyramids of Ancient Egypt intended for older junior children is written in a fairly formal way:

> Since the Egyptians believed that the dead man returned each day to the chapel, gifts of food and drink were left for him. The chamber to which he would return was most wonderfully decorated and furnished. (Unstead 1959)

The initial part of the first sentence is long and contains an explanation which the reader has to absorb before reaching the main clause or real information of the sentence – that food and drink was left for the dead man. In addition, this description is written in the third person making the register more formal.

As pupils come to key stages 3 and 4, they will read an increased number of text books. A major task of the transitional period between junior and secondary school is the development of readers' earlier experience of listening to, writing and reading more formal texts. We might, at this point, directly intervene and make sure that readers understand the meaning of a sentence such as:

> In battles which continually took place over the centuries, an army holding the crossing place at Cambridge was in a very strong position to repel its enemy. (Graham-Cameron 1977)

We might ask readers to underline the most important part of the sentence and to discuss their decision. Such activity may be on a group or individual basis.

Readers may have a further difficulty as they read this sentence from the same book, 'Gradually, houses were built beside this fording place and much later, a bridge was built' (Graham-Cameron 1977). If pupils are to read this sentence for information efficiently, they must comprehend that ancient peoples built the bridges and houses. Such understanding may depend upon the teacher pointing out the inference within the sentence and the link to information which has already been given.

Of course, teachers cannot undertake such activities whenever readers are confronted by complex sentences, but readers should have some kind of strategy to hand when they try to read increasingly difficult texts.

We discussed abstract language in Chapter 3 as another possible aspect of the mode. It is a characteristic feature of more formal books. When readers begin to seek information from books, they will almost certainly be confronted by this kind of language. Consider the following statement: 'The Permian reptiles on this page lived on into the Triassic period in some cases, but then their age died out' (Leutscher 1971).

Precisely how will a young reader interpret *their age*? Common use of *their age* does not have quite the same meaning. Young readers will probably read the phrase fluently but may well not understand its import. If we do not assist readers to become familiar with such phraseology, they will have less chance of developing as readers who can manage texts such as:

> Still, while man fears the predators, he secretly exults in their power, he feels a contagion, an emotional kinship to them. It is no coincidence that visitors to the African parks watch not the impala and zebra, but the lion and leopard. Even in sleep these big cats convey a feeling of barely contained strength, an ever-present threat of death, which man the hunter finds satisfying, though the danger is vicarious from the safety of a car. Our dual past still haunts us. We hear a lion roar and the primate in us shivers; we see huge herds of game and the predator in us is delighted, as if our existence still depended on their presence. (McSweeney and Debes 1975).

Will our readers understand *emotional kinship*, *barely contained strength*, *man the hunter*, *our dual past*, *primate in us*, *predator in us*? It may be argued that readers will not understand these phrases until they have the cognitive ability to appreciate abstraction and such ability may not develop until pupils are well into the secondary school. However, Christie (1985a) points out that many of the problems of young readers are linguistic rather than cognitive.

Key stages 3 and 4 (ages 11/12 to 14 and 14–16)
(travel books, consumer reports, text books, contrasts, information leaflets, publicity material, newspapers, magazines, advertisements, leader columns, pressure group literature)

In the early years of the secondary school, some pupils may still read expository books which are written in a more personal tenor as in the following extract:

> So far, you have seen machines used to harvest grain and grass. There are many other crops, and different machines are used to harvest them. (Wykeham 1979)

The print used in this book is fairly large and each page contains a large diagram. This is perfectly reasonable, so long as it is appreciated that pupils should also meet books written far more formally.

At key stage 4, pupils will read more advanced text books in which these register characteristics of expository writing become increasingly evident. Teachers often dismiss such writing as being too formal for their pupils and would agree with Hull in despairing that most school text books are produced 'as if in the spirit of irony especially for educational purposes' (1985: 213). We will take a far more positive view if we consider it to be part of reading development. For instance, if pupils are to develop some understanding of the way in which subject specializations are studied and reported, then they must gradually be introduced to books where the register is characteristic of the way a subject is written about.

Different subjects are expressed in specific ways, for as knowledge about various subjects has developed, so has the form in which language expresses those ideas. For instance, there are specific, independent ways of writing about geographical, historical and scientific thinking.

In an Australian study of history text books (Eggins *et al.* 1987), the researchers suggest that historians select, interpret and generalize from facts about the past. We should constantly remind ourselves that history is not a fictional story although it is sometimes suggested as such to young children. In more advanced history texts people are often not represented as individuals. People may be mentioned as characterizing the kind of thinking or activity of a particular period. Historians often remove people altogether from their accounts and create distance between past events and readers by the use of abstract and figurative language. Such may be the language of history text books which older secondary pupils meet.

Geography is written about in quite a different way from history. Again, Eggins *et al* report that geographers have to group and classify where and what things or places are. They must analyse and explain how things are caused and how they affect other things. These purposes are different from those of historians who select, interpret and generalize about the past. Eggins *et al* explain that technical vocabulary is inevitably used by geographers to name and define aspects of the world. Taxonomies are set up as a way of organizing the world. This kind of organization is also used by writers about science. Both geography and scientific writers have to define and explain terms.

We can show pupils how authors of science text books often make great use of the passive voice because they are writing about natural phenomena in a detached way. We can point out that these writers wish to explain scientific facts without allowing their personal responses to intrude as in this sentence: 'After the ammonia has been removed by reducing the temperature and causing it to liquefy, the other gases are recycled' (Hart 1978). Pupils may think of this as boring and thus the teacher should be prepared to share with those readers the reasons why specialist writing is organized in particular ways. Even chapter headings and sub-headings can be pointed out as indicating the way in which the writer is ordering the content of the chapter or book. For instance, the chapter heading 'Ocean currents' obviously states that ocean currents are to be described. The word *current* is used repeatedly and there is explanation of its meaning, 'Currents are great bands of water moving through the oceans' (Jennings 1988).

Even within that sentence, the word *bands* may suggest a very different subject area than that of ocean currents. Many junior children may have limited experience of the use of *currents* and *bands* outside of the everyday meanings of *currant* as a dried fruit and *band* as a musical band. Thus whilst we may feel that content is the least problematic of the aspects of register, it can hold dangers for comprehension.

We must be aware that subject texts will contain many content words which will increase the problems of understanding. Many writers explain quite complex new ideas in relatively few words. Obviously, as the text becomes more technical, this *packed meaning* will confront the reader. Many reference books eagerly taken by readers undertaking projects contain many content words, as in this book about the universe:

> Stars are the units or **building blocks** of even larger star systems known as **galaxies**. Our own sun is only one star in a huge galaxy containing over one hundred billion stars. And this is not all. Beyond our galaxy there are billions of other galaxies which make up the building blocks of the **universe**. (Brown 1984)

As we saw in Chapter 3, if we count the number of content words against the number of words which are purely grammatical, we will be more aware of the reading difficulty involved. Consider the demands made upon pupils' understanding as they read these extracts:

> Energy is transferred by infra-red rays which can travel through a vacuum, at the speed of light. Dull black surfaces are good radiators and good absorbers. (Pople 1982)

> As you can see from the equation, the reaction is reversible and the gases emerging from the reaction chamber contain unreacted nitrogen and hydrogen. (Hart 1978)

Further, Christie (1985a) reminds us that a scientific expository text book does not include opinions. It is *a matter of fact* and it is written with the intention that pupils must come to understand it. So here is a difficult reading purpose which requires assistance from the teacher.

Language of persuasion At key stage 2, pupils are to think about the language of advertisements. Many advertisements might be placed in the procedural genre but we will consider them all under this heading.

It is mainly, however, at key stage 4, that pupils are judged ready to read the kind of information which is so common in adult life. Level 6 states that readers should be able to 'recognise in discussion, whether subject matter in non-literary and media texts is presented as fact or as an opinion'. Awareness of register can go a long way to helping us understand how writers use language in order to persuade readers.

Argument is really more common in speech than in writing. Kress (1989) lists debate, discussion, argument and quarrel as familiar forms of spoken argument. Unless we give pupils experience of the way in which argument is written, they will write argument in a register which is more appropriate to spoken language and then their work is less valued.

It is interesting to note that the text books which older pupils read are usually more concerned with information than with argument. Older pupils, however, probably write more argument in history, geography and science lessons than in English lessons as Freedman and Pringle (1989) suggest. Consequently, they may eventually manage to write argument more easily in these more structured lessons than they do in English lessons. This is where reading and writing have to be closely inter-related if we are to help pupils appreciate written argument.

We should also note how some journalists use the language of spoken argument as they write their articles. In the following leader article from the *Sun* newspaper, the writer has even used underlining in order to draw attention first to the unlikely greeting of, *Cheers, Bish* and then to emphasize the opinion of the writer. In fact, our reading is almost directed. We can also indicate to our pupils the informality of the language and its close relationship to everyday spoken language.

> **Cheers, Bish**
> The Bishop of —— is in trouble because he takes a pint at his local.
>
> The local temperance league say he should spend less time in the pub and more in the pulpit.
>
> But he's far more likely to find out down the local what concerns ordinary folk than he is if he's confined to. . . (leading article: *Sun*, 21 October 1989)

Awareness of tenor, that is the degree of formality, will help us to analyse advertisements with our pupils. The following advertisement for financial loans (*Sunday Times*, 10 December 1989) clearly speaks to the reader:

> Send off the coupon and get a cheque back in the post. Could it really be that painless?
>
> If you're a homeowner it could be. There are no interviews. No legal fees. No hanging around for the answer . . . .

Leaders from quality newspapers may provide pupils with examples of arguments which are well presented. An argument is written to prove a point and thus the writer explains the *thesis* or main point and gives examples to back up the claim being made. Freedman and Pringle (1989) point out that we should provide models so that older readers can perceive the difference between a well-constructed argument and persuasive writing such as we find in advertisements, pressure group literature and publicity material of all kinds.

Reading different types of procedural writing

Authors of books which I categorize as being in the procedural genre, wish to instruct pupils in some kind of activity. Usually, they give step-by-step instructions, and therefore, the form of writing is reasonably distinct. The tenor is fairly formal because there are commands. We tend to assume that readers will understand this genre of writing, yet they will meet all kinds of register variation within procedural writing.

Key stage 1 (ages 5–7)
(notices, books of instructions)

Young pupils can be encouraged to find out instructions and information by reading displayed notices. These notices should be written so that the instructions are clearly set out and provide a good model of this kind of writing. We can ensure that we select instruction books for young readers, which again are clearly set out.

Key stage 2 (ages 7–11)

It is surprising that there are no suggestions for reading procedural texts at this stage. My survey (Appendix 2) suggested that many such texts are read by pupils at this stage.

Frequently, older junior school pupils work from number books and language books in which they are coping with quite different register features, such as technical signs and numbers. For instance, different type may be used for emphasis and varied technical signs may be introduced, particularly in mathematics and science books. Authors may well change the register patterning within a set of instructions. This change in itself may cause confusion but if we are aware of it ourselves, then we can indicate to pupils why this change occurs.

In this extract from a book about health, the author writes in the procedural genre: 'Write a heading FOOD AND GROWING, and leave half a page in your book. Fill in the answers when you have them' (Johnson and Williams 1980). The writers then change to a register which is more characteristic of writing in the expository genre: 'You could also find out what food you were given as a toddler and why. Remember you couldn't talk to ask for foods even if you had known what you needed!'

Perhaps you can note the change in register patterning. First the writers instruct by writing a command. They then use the model verb *could* which simply suggests rather than orders the pupil to do something. This is followed by an explanation as to why you would have to ask for the information rather than remember it. In fact, the expository writing continues with increasing complexity:

> When you are talking to your family or your teacher about food, or looking at special books about it, you may come across some words which help to describe the sort of things which foods contain and which the body needs.

Here, we have another example of a very long introduction to the main information in the sentence: 'You may come across some words.' The linking within the sentence is complicated. The sentence begins with a conjunction *when*. The main clause of the sentence is qualified yet again by three further clauses each joined by the tie *which*. This is a great deal of complexity to assimilate as a reader. Perhaps our main task as a teacher here is to recognize that difficulty and to highlight the instructions.

> *Key stages 3 and 4 (ages 11/12 to 14 and 14–16)*
> (guide books, sets of instructions, manuals, stage
> directions, forms, the highway code)

A range of procedural writing is suggested in *English for Ages 5 to 16* (DES 1989) at this stage. We might also note that many sections of text books are written in the procedural genre. Again, instructions may be presented in a paragraph and the reader has to be able to note the list-like structure of the paragraph as in this extract:

> Sink a jar into the soil. Put a square of card over the top to keep out rain. Use bits of wood to hold the card above the ground. Put two pitfall traps in the school grounds. (Hill and Holman 1986)

Clearly, this extract should not be read in the same way as a story, but do your slower readers know that? It can only be helpful to young readers if the purposes of the writer are pointed out. Perhaps it would be helpful to many readers if they highlighted each instruction.

Sometimes subject-specialist teachers complain that their pupils cannot read. Here is argument that every subject teacher should be in a position to recognize difficulties which the language of their subject may give to some readers. Most mathematics text books are written as instructions, but another register may also be introduced by the writer:

> D3 There are two points on the map which are exactly 50 km from the Radio Barset transmitter and exactly 40 km from the Radio Arcady transmitter. Mark them A and B on your map. (*SMP* 11–16 Bk B3)

Again, we might well take the time to analyse with our pupils, the information and then the instruction. The description has to be understood precisely. This means that the cohesive tie *which* has to be related to *two points* and the two points to the two transmitters. Here may be a case for rough diagrammatic representation of the meaning of the sentence before the instruction is answered.

When we ask pupils to work from mathematics books or language skills books etc., I do not think that we always realize that those pupils may face a demanding reading task. This difficulty might well be alleviated if we explain to pupils how the language of the instructions is ordered and relate that organization to the task itself.

This tendency to introduce more than one register is a feature of school text books and of explanatory and instructional writing in general. The writers of travel guides, for instance, may move from description of places to instructions about travel.

The Egyptian Museum, Cairo

The Egyptian national museum for Pharaonic antiquities was created by Said Pasha in 1857, at the urging of the Egyptologist Auguste Mariette. The original building, in the suburb of Bulaq, could not contain the growing collection, which in 1890 was moved to a palace in Giza, and finally to the Tahir Square, constructed by the architect Marcel Dourgnon in 1897–1902. . . . *Hours: daily 9 am to 4 pm (closed Fridays 11.30 am to 1.30 pm)* (Murnane 1983).

We can point out to readers that, in this case, the writer has signalled the change of purpose by using italics.

Familiarity with the register of writing in the procedural genre may well help older readers to follow the format of forms which they have to complete. Of course, manuals or stage directions will probably be read with the purpose of completing a task. The register of this genre is very much the language of action rather than of reflection.

Reading different types of reference writing

The purpose of the author who writes in the reference genre is to provide concise information about specific subjects in some kind of sequential way as, on the whole, these books are used for reference. The books are characterised by the overall pattern of a list which is usually dependent upon some kind of taxonomy: alphabetical, as in a dictionary or in some encyclopedia, or to do with particular subjects.

Key stage 1 (ages 5–7)
(plans, maps, diagrams, computer printouts, dictionaries,
word books, computer data, road signs, logos)

It is recommended that young pupils begin at this stage to look at diagrammatic reference material such as plans and maps. Thus, we must expand our initial definition to include types of writing where there may be other means of representing meaning besides using words. Maps and plans require understanding of a different kind. In fact, some pupils will probably require constant explanation of this kind of writing throughout their school careers. We must not assume that readers implicitly comprehend the way that understanding is represented within diagrams.

We have also to make sure that our young readers understand the way their first dictionaries and word books are set out. These initial explanations will help future flexibility of reading ability.

Key stage 2 (ages 7–11)
(lists of contents, indexes, library classification, library
catalogue, advertisements)

Junior school libraries vary in the way in which books are classified. However, pupils at this stage should, at least, be aware that fiction and non-fiction are classified separately; that fiction is classified in alphabetical order of the author's surname; that non-fiction is classified by subject.

Pupils of this age usually undertake topic work and refer to a range of information. Many information books used in project work, both in the junior and secondary school, contain lists such as indexes and lists of contents. Again, we cannot assume that all pupils will be able to use these reference devices. Pupils should be able to see the relationship between the index and list of contents and the text.

Far too many reference books contain either poor reference strategies or none at all. It may be that it is very difficult to find a reasonable amount of information on the page indicated. As we have already noted, illustrations may not relate to the written text which appears on the same page. These kind of problems make needless difficulties for readers of all ages. Perhaps the best strategy for teachers is to be highly selective in buying new information books, for publishers are swift to react to the perceived needs of teachers.

In the course of topic work, pupils may well use encyclopedia and dictionaries although these types of reference writing are not indicated until stages 3 and 4. Again, as pupils refer to these reference sources, they should be aware that the register used to define items in an encyclopedia is often expository and that it can be quite complex as in this extract:

In these (mills) the whole mill, including its machinery and sails, is carried by a box-like house which is mounted on a central vertical post, on which it can be turned so that the sails face into the wind. (Wright 1976a).

In this sentence, vocabulary which is probably reasonably familiar to pupils, is expressed in a complex way. There are many cohesive ties where the meaning has to be linked to an item which has been previously mentioned – *these, its, it, which, on which.* There is, therefore, considerable likelihood for confusion in the reader's mind.

Dictionaries contain an unusual register. Quite often the compiler does not write the definition of words in sentences but in phrases which will be unusual for many readers. Sometimes more than one meaning of a word may be given depending on the context in which the word is used – again, something which needs explanation.

This junior dictionary expresses meaning in a reasonably simplified way:

nib The metal point of a pen (Wright 1976b).

Compare this extract from the adult *Concise Oxford Dictionary*:

loom v.i. & n. 1. Appear indistinctly, to be seen in vague and often magnified or threatening shape, (lit. & fig.; often large etc.)

The vocabulary of the latter extract is probably less familiar to the reader. There are many abbreviations which indicate the different uses of the words. Even if we do not wish to explain fully their importance, we might say something to our pupils about the reasons why those abbreviations appear.

So, just because we know that our readers are able to follow the mechanics of looking up a word in a dictionary, we should not assume that all those readers can understand the abbreviations and explanations they will find there.

Key stages 3 and 4 (ages 11/12 to 14 and 14–16)
(dictionaries, thesauruses, encyclopediae, subject reference
books, adult encyclopediae, data bases)

Readers' reference material becomes increasingly sophisticated but we can offer continual assistance, particularly by making pupils aware of the kind of aids (list of contents, indexes) which they should seek within reference books.

In addition, pupils can be encouraged to search for information in more sophisticated ways. If pupils at this stage have not had the opportunity to use an organized library, it is essential that they are introduced to the basic structure of a library. Secondary school libraries will probably have systems of cards which form the library catalogue. Pupils can become familiar with subject catalogues, title catalogues and author catalogues. In some libraries, a computer system may be used and teaching about how to cope with this technology is clearly necessary.

As pupils read more books for information, they will discover that not all writing in the reference genre is organized in some sort of chronological order, but rather as a logical structure as noted in *English for Ages 5 to 16* (DES 1989: 16.40). This may be true of some subject reference books and of data bases.

Increasing use of computers indicates the importance of pupils becoming familiar with the various forms in which information is organized in a computer data bank. In fact, we might say that writing in the reference genre is rapidly becoming of the greatest importance as information technology develops in schools.

Summary

It is helpful to categorize into genres the types of writing proposed in the recommendations for the National Curriculum in reading. Knowledge of the linguistic choices which authors make as they compose the different registers of the language of these genres indicates something of the range of writing and its increasing complexity with which pupils are to become familiar as they grow older.

Linguistically informed junior and secondary school teachers are in a position to intervene helpfully in pupils' reading when they judge it to be appropriate.

CHAPTER 5

Some pupils' awareness of register

We know that even very young children are able to speak in different registers. One has only to listen to a 3-year-old speak to a small baby or note that most children do not speak to their teacher in the same way as they speak to their friends in the playground. Children are part of the social environment and as such become implicitly aware of the most obvious changes in spoken registers. However, they do not have the same experience of the use of different registers in written language.

The research

We have little knowledge of how children develop an awareness of different registers or what part is played by such awareness in the development of their reading. A research project was therefore designed (Littlefair 1988) to try to find some indications which might help us to understand more about this.

It is difficult to devise a way of surveying pupils' awareness of register. Register is an abstract concept and it is therefore not reasonable to try to discuss register as such with the majority of pupils. I decided, however, to create a situation in the school in which pupils could discuss differences between texts which we would look at together. I wanted to encourage pupils to expand their own ideas rather than be prompted by me. By having individual discussions, I hoped that all the pupils would feel that they could attempt the task without fear of failure. In addition, this kind of task would be flexible enough to use with pupils of different ages and abilities.

Selection of pupils

With the help of their teachers, I selected 72 children to take part in the research. Of these, 24 children came from each of four 3rd-year junior school classes, two 1st-year secondary school classes and two 4th-year secondary school classes.

The children were of different reading abilities which I categorized as: less able readers, average readers, able readers. We decided to use the Gap and Gapadol tests as objective measures of reading ability. The *Gap* (McLeod 1970) reading comprehension test is based on the cloze procedure and is designed for use with junior school pupils. The *Gapadol* (McLeod and Anderson 1973) reading comprehension test is also based on the cloze procedure but is designed for use with 1st-year secondary school pupils. Cloze procedure requires readers to suggest words for deletions which have been systematically made in a text. In order to balance the possible inaccuracy of the testing, I was able to discuss the placing of pupils within ability groups with their teachers. I did not include non-readers nor children whose first language was not English so as not to compromise the findings. Also, it seemed to me more reasonable to refer to 4th-year secondary school pupils as less able pupils, average pupils and able pupils rather than readers since all these pupils were said to read competently. I selected 4th-year secondary school pupils for these groups on the basis of the results predicted for them in the GCSE examinations and from discussion with teachers.

Register break activity

I did not wish to plunge children of any age straight into a discussion about language issues and so I devised an introductory task to give the readers some idea of what I meant when I talked about comparing pages from different books.

Each age group of readers was given a page of *puzzles* which consisted of brief passages taken from books of different genres. In each passage, a word or phrase was changed to a word or phrase written in a different register. First, we looked at a practice passage which we solved together and then the readers were asked to underline words or groups of words which they considered had been altered into a 'different kind of writing' in a similar way. Examples of the register break puzzles are to be found in Appendix 3.

This strategy proved to be an effective way of talking about language variety and promised to be a method which might well be used in the classroom, particularly as pupils discuss with each other where there might be an appropriate use of language.

The individual discussions

As each pupil arrived for our discussion, I placed four pages, each from a book in a major genre category, on a table. I explained that I wanted the pupil to help me organize 12 other pages into the categories suggested by the first four examples. Of course, pages were selected which were appropriate for the different age groups of pupils involved. As the individual readers compared each of the pages with the displayed four pages, they gave a reason(s) for choosing the page which seemed to them to be most similar. Sometimes their reason was brief, sometimes non-existent, but sometimes it was fairly involved. The readers referred to varied aspects of the pages: the content, the vocabulary, the way the language was expressed, and the purpose of the writer. This discussion was just as much to do with language as it was to do with the content of the pages. Needless to say, not all responses were so coherent but all the responses had some bearing on the problem of how far young readers are aware of the register of texts which they read.

As I listened to the tape recordings which I made of these discussions, I was able to group the responses as shown in Table 2.

Table 2 Categories of pupils' responses

No awareness of register
matching pages by chance
unreasonable link suggested between pages
Some awareness of register
illustrations noted
tenuous relationships between pages noted
narrative not noted
What is being written about?
content of page wrongly indicated
content of page indicated correctly
page recognized from a previous reading
page seen as belonging to a particular subject category
How is the page written?
one linguistic characteristic noted
mention made of the language used
more detailed description/comparison of language used
Who is the page written for? The attitude of the author
some mention of the formality or tone of the writer
Purpose of the author
author's purpose indicated correctly
intuition claimed
author's purpose described in detail
Not relevant
no choice made
sees dissimilarities between pages only

I noted each response as an example of one of these sub-groupings. It was possible to compare the number of responses in one category with those in another category. This is not a statistical survey, but it is revealing to look at the trends of the responses.

Trends of the responses

Basic problems of the readers

All the pupils understood that they were to match different pages into groups. The task of categorization itself was not a problem for all pupils made some attempt to sort the pages. The difficulties which arose seemed to be linguistic rather than cognitive for, in order to manage this task, the pupils really had to look at similarities in vocabulary, grammar and other graphic features.

Some readers said they were just guessing as they categorized the pages. Others said they had no idea why they had placed a page in a particular category. A few readers did not respond at all after they had categorized a page. Most of the pupils who responded in this way were less able 3rd-year readers but we should note that they were not considered to be non-readers.

Sometimes as pupils looked for a possible link between pages, they made unreasonable suggestions. For example, one less able 3rd-year junior school reader looked at the sketch of a baby on a page about health care and decided that page should go with a page describing hurricanes but which included the drawing of an aeroplane, because as he said, 'There's a baby there and he can see it going overhead.' Another 3rd-year junior school reader placed a page from a dictionary with a page from a book about health which contained an illustration of a baby. The reason given was, 'Their children learn to read and they need to look at those when they write things and it's got all these words in it they need.' Another reader thought that a page from a book about Saxons could be grouped with a page from a book on Ancient Egypt because the Saxons 'probably lived in there' (the pyramid).

These pupils' explanations have little to do with the language on the pages but they have to do with ideas suggested by looking at the pages. Many of these responses also suggested that these children had difficulty in articulating their reasons. Perhaps they had more difficulty than others in being able to conceptualize. It might also be that their introduction to literacy has not been very rich and therefore they have not enough experience to allow them to interpret the task with more understanding.

Figure 1 shows the large number of less able 3rd-year junior school readers who seemed unable to respond to the linguistic implications of the task which I had set them. It is important to note that this lack of linguistic awareness seems to mirror lower reading ability. It may be argued that the fact that these readers did not really refer to the linguistic expression on the pages cannot be related to reading development. However, Figure 1 suggests that average and able readers did not give these kinds of vague responses. Some less able readers, however, did so even in the 1st- and 4th-year groups in the secondary schools. Most of these basic difficulties seem to disappear in the secondary school which suggests a development of register awareness as children widen their experience of written language.

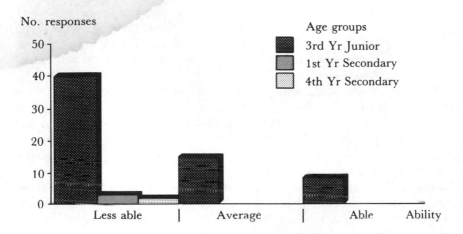

Figure 1: Readers with no awareness of register

Readers who have some awareness of register

It was most apparent in the junior school that readers seemed to indicate a gradual development of awareness of differing register features of the pages they were discussing. At first, pupils looked for content. This is to be expected since we discuss with pupils the meaning of stories they read. Other genres of writing do not afford the same clues from the dynamics of a plot and other clues to meaning are sought. Perhaps the first and most obvious clue comes from illustrations. We have already seen that less able pupils, in particular, jump to all kinds of strange conclusions about the meaning of a text which are based on illustrations. There does seem to come a stage, however, when young readers have more positive interpretations of illustrations although the author's meaning is only partly understood. One reader compared a page from a book about Saxons with one about Ancient Egyptians: 'because they're working. I saw pick axes.

On page 1, they're building a pyramid.' This kind of response was only made by junior school readers. Perhaps getting clues from pictures and illustrations only is a feature of the young reader rather than the less able reader.

These responses suggested that pupils were looking for similar features on different pages but were still not really aware of the language used by the authors. Even able 3rd-year junior school readers were not always able to look beyond the content area of the page, particularly when they looked at pages taken from books across the curriculum. Able readers did not make these kind of responses in the 1st or 4th year of the secondary school but less able readers did!

A less able 1st-year secondary school reader compared a map of agriculture in the UK with a page from a local history book, 'It's sort of like the olden days. Farming and tractors – they're not like we have now.' A less able 4th-year pupil looked at a page from a typing manual and noted, 'Typewriters have to do with English.'

I was surprised that some pupils did not seem to recognize a story, for most children have experience of stories from a very early age and so it is not surprising that the majority of pupils had little difficulty in noting the pages of fiction. However, some less able pupils did not seem to recognize narrative. Even in a 1st-year secondary school group, a less able reader placed a page from a narrative with a page from a history book, 'Because it's got a "soldier" here and that's got a picture of soldiers.' Perhaps these pupils who were not aware that a page came from a story had little experience of books. If this is the case, then understanding of other book genres will be a problem.

We should not assume that even able junior school readers are always aware of the meaning of texts from different genres. Figure 2 suggests that this stage of awareness of language variety is mainly to be found in the junior school but that some readers still have little awareness even in the secondary school. So even allowing able junior school readers to work independently with books from different genres may not be so straightforward an activity as we might have thought.

Awareness of content (field)

Jumping to wrong conclusions Few readers described the contents of a page inaccurately. Sometimes readers made assumptions about the content of a text on the basis of a single word. This suggests that those pupils were only looking at a single feature of the language. It does seem reasonable that we should help those pupils to be aware of other linguistic features which the author has used.

Most teachers will be aware of this kind of error which has disastrous

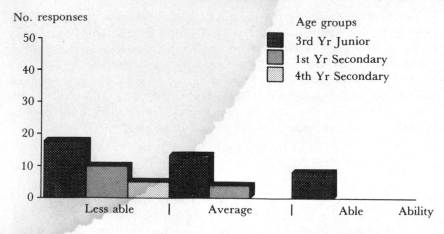

Figure 2: Readers with some awareness of register

implications for understanding: an average 3rd-year junior school reader described a page of instructions for writing tasks as coming from a story book because of the word 'stories' which appears in the first sentence. Even an average 1st-year secondary school reader looked at a map of agricultural products and declared, 'It's about history. It's a map and that. History is about maps.' Clearly, we cannot know all the preconceptions which a pupil may have but equally we cannot assume that they are not present.

Certainly there was no evidence of this kind of mis-reading given by 1st- and 4th-year secondary school able readers who often reserved judgement about the topic of a page until they had skimmed a little of the text. However, the problem of jumping to the wrong conclusions about the field of a text increased in the responses of less competent 4th-year secondary school pupils. At this stage, pupils are reading more difficult texts across the curriculum. If they misunderstand the general topic of the book, the readers will not understand the text and possibly declare the book unintelligible.

Noting the content correctly   On the other hand, there were many perceptive comments by readers about the content of a page. An average 3rd-year reader looked at a page taken from *The Otterbury Incident* by C. Day Lewis and declared, 'I think it's more adventurous. It's sort of like when they have adventure stories, they always start off good and all of these have started off good and they're adventurous.' It is interesting to note that more able readers reserved judgement about the topic of a page until they had skimmed a little of the text.

An able 4th-year reader looked at a page taken from a book about computers: 'It's factual again. I started at the first sentence or so and looked over the page. I didn't understand what they were at first until I started reading that and I realised it was about computers.'

At the other extreme, I only had one response from less able 3rd-year junior school readers which indicated a correct interpretation of the content. We might suspect that young less able readers have greater difficulties of understanding than we might imagine.

Identifying text as from a specialist subject.   Not very many junior school readers suggested that pages belonged to subject areas of the curriculum. This is not really surprising since junior school timetables tend to be integrated. However, a considerable number of 1st-year secondary school pupils referred to different pages as belonging to particular subject areas. Perhaps we are seeing here one effect of the sudden appearance of a subject dominated timetable. Readers seem to begin to associate their school books with the subject and possibly with the teacher of that subject.

This kind of response from less able readers in the 4th year of the secondary school increased. So a less able 4th-year pupil described a page from a reference book about fish in this way: 'Fish has got something to do with biology.'

The same kind of responses actually decreased from the able and average 4th-year secondary school readers. These readers seemed to pay comparatively little attention to categorizing the pages they reviewed into subject areas. They concentrated on other aspects of the language used by the authors of the individual pages. Here is a striking difference in emphasis: more able 4th-year secondary school pupils do not seem to regard books as being simply part of a subject area but they are more aware of the meaning of the text itself. Figure 3 shows the quite striking trends of these kinds of responses.

Readers look at how language is used (mode)

Noting a single linguistic feature   Some readers from each junior school ability group indicated that a single characteristic of the language of the text suggested to them the genre of writing. We have already noted that young readers are, on the whole, extremely familiar with story. Most children's stories contain conversation and this feature was particularly noted. An average 3rd-year junior school reader remarked, 'It's a story. It's got speech marks because people are talking.' A less able reader in a 1st-year secondary school group explained, 'It seems sort of like a story, the same because them speech marks go around.' A 4th-year average reader

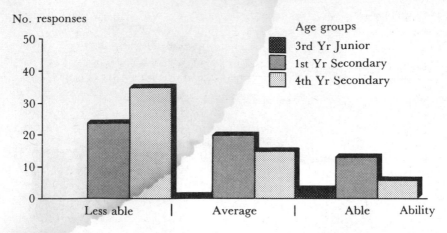

Figure 3: Readers identify text as from a specialist subject

categorized a page as a story because of, 'the punctuation. As you look at it, you can see the punctuation on it.'

Sometimes, as the readers looked at the pages from other genres of books, they mentioned similarity of numbering or lettering or of the title. A 3rd-year average junior school reader noted, 'Usually in story books, they have the name of the story and the name of the chapter at the top.'

Noting further features of languages   Some readers were able to comment a little further about the way in which authors used language. They were becoming aware that there is some kind of pattern in particular books. The pattern might be to do with language or with the kind of print used or with diagrams or technical signs.

Many responses referred to pages from stories but there was also evidence of a development, for some readers began to note the more obvious ways in which language is used by authors of other genres of books. An average 3rd-year junior school reader saw the pattern of a reference book. 'It's different animals and that's different birds and they've got little paragraphs about each of them.' A 1st-year secondary school reader compared a page from a reference book and a page from a play: 'They've got the names on the left and they've got the writing on the other side.'

In the 4th year of a secondary school, an average pupil looked at a page of fiction and said, 'It's a story book I should think. The actual paragraphing. You can see that's a book because there's people talking with one another and there's detailed paragraphs.'

Figure 4 suggests that there is fairly consistent development of readers' awareness of the more obvious ways in which authors use language.

No. responses

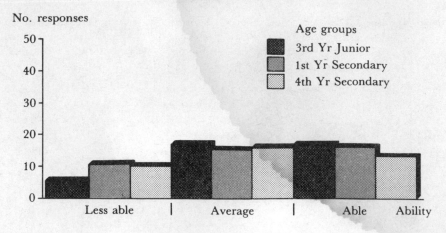

Figure 4: Readers note a simple linguistic feature

Looking at language in more detail   There does seem to be far more rapid development of awareness by able readers of the more complex ways in which language is used by authors. For example, an able 3rd-year junior school reader refers to a page where the author is describing hurricanes, 'That's sort of scientific like this one. It's explaining something. The language it uses. You wouldn't in a story, or something like that, say, "Hurricanes appear over the Caribbean and other parts of the world." '

As we will discuss later in more detail, both narrative and history may be written about in a similar register. It is obvious that readers should note the similarity and yet understand the relevant purposes of the authors. Thus it is an able 3rd-year junior school reader who notes, 'They're both stories which tell you about things but they are in a kind of story sort of way but it's kind of fact. It is written as a story but it tells you things what have happened.'

Whenever less able readers mainly showed this kind of awareness, they were usually looking at pages taken from narrative and their responses were often less articulate as this response suggests. 'A guess because it's the same thing. The same kind of typing. It's all story written with all the speech marks and things.'

We must assume that the able readers developed this kind of awareness without specific teaching. Again, we should note the influence of the wider experience of genres which occurs in the 1st year of the secondary school. A 1st-year secondary school reader described the language used in a description of dinosaurs.

It's an information book. It's purely giving you information about, in this case, dinosaurs. Instead of saying Chapter 7 or something like that, it's got the heading 'Dinosaurs' and then it gives you information. There's no speech marks something like this, but they lay it out in paragraphs about different things. There are pictures in it to describe like this.

Many of these able readers were very articulate. For example, a 1st-year able secondary school reader describes a dictionary, 'That's a dictionary. The words it's talking about are thickly written so it stands out and then it sometimes has sort of Latin or something and then it explains the word.'

Another able 1st-year secondary school reader compared a description of early Christianity with a page from a narrative.

In here, it said, 'In AD 64'. It's describing something. This is describing something as well but in a different way. That one's just describing a situation to you where you then get the characters speaking and saying what's happened and here you're just getting a description of what was happening then.

By contrast, a less able 4th-year secondary school reader attempted to describe two pages from instructional books: 'That's telling you how to make something. It's got diagrams. It's the same setting out.'

So many of the readers who are represented in Figure 5 indicated an ability to describe and compare in greater detail the way in which the author had used language or diagrams, illustrations or print. The degree to which the able 1st-year secondary school readers seemed to have developed this ability is most striking and is in sharp contrast to even the average readers in the same age group.

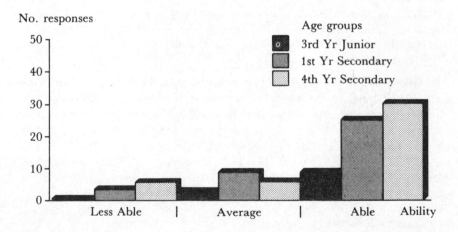

Figure 5: Readers note more detailed linguistic features

We now have to consider whether the ability to read well goes hand in hand with the development of awareness of the different ways in which authors use language. Certainly, readers in the average and less able groups really show little development of this kind of awareness. Any responses which gave this kind of information were usually concerned with narrative texts. From this evidence, it would seem that most readers would benefit from some explicit teaching about the way in which other genres are written.

Looking at the formality of language (tenor)

Few readers made comments which referred to the way in which writers make clear their attitudes to their readers or to the content. This is not surprising because it is very difficult to explain how authors are able to write in a way which is formal as opposed to being informal.

Some pupils were able to relate the degree of formality or informality of a page they were discussing to a similar tenor of language in another book or within another situation in their experience. For example, a less able junior school reader spoke about a page from a story book, 'I think it's another story. It says here, "Don't you know...." It's like a dad or mum saying to a child.' An able reader in the same age group remarked:

> I read that kind of book at home so I know they are fiction stories. That's more kind of children's style – talking. That's exactly the way children would read, say things like, 'Get up idiot'.

The few pertinent responses from junior school pupils were mainly concerned with the familiar tenor of narrative, although an able reader noted an unusual tenor in a story book:

> This one's a story book and it's sort of not modern, neither is this. It's about before now – just sounds like it. 'A thin high shouldered shadow flickered grotesquely on the wall behind him.' You wouldn't use that type of language if it were modern times.

Genres other than narrative usually are far more formal and it is this formality of language which causes so many problems of understanding. Few readers were as perceptive as this 1st-year secondary school reader who noted the appropriate formality of the language of an expository book about dinosaurs: 'That's history. It's facts. It's no story line in it. It's realistic rather than silly things like him saying, "Hello" to another dinosaur.' Yet again, here is an aspect of the language used by authors which we might well point out to our developing readers.

Looking at authors' purposes

Readers in all the age and ability groups showed some awareness of the immediate purposes of authors. Probably, they associated these purposes with those of the lessons in which they used the books. There was, however, markedly less awareness of this kind by less able 3rd-year junior school readers.

An average junior school reader described a page about division:

> That's telling you about maths and it's telling you an easier way how to work it out. It's just telling you at the beginning, 'For each of these regular polygons find out the length of one side.... It's giving you a clue how to measure them.

Again, the less able junior school pupils did not show as much awareness as other readers.

This sense of the purpose increases in the responses of the less able and average readers in the 1st year of the secondary school. Once more, this may well be the result of experiencing the subject-dominated timetable of the secondary school. An average 1st-year secondary school reader described the purpose of a book about calculators, 'It's like learning things like you learn how to use a calculator and sort of experiments.'

Some readers stated the purpose of an author of a page they were reading almost intuitively as did this able 3rd-year reader, 'It's reference: scientific and reference books. It just feels right to go with that one.'

Figure 6 shows how the number of relevant responses by the average 1st- and 4th-year secondary school readers increased. On the other hand, those on the 4th-year less able pupils do not differ greatly from the number noted by the less able 1st-year secondary school readers. Clearly food for

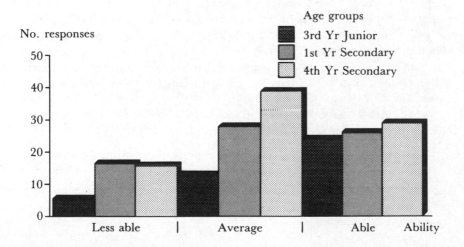

Figure 6: Readers note authors' purposes

thought although it should be noted that I was talking to a fairly small number of pupils.

Looking at detailed author's purposes   No 3rd-year junior school reader made a comment which suggested awareness of authors' detailed purposes. This is the only category of responses where there is such a lack of comment which suggests that we are discussing a complex issue.

As pupils increasingly understand the purpose of authors, so they will increasingly understand that authors have to construct their meanings in different ways. This kind of awareness signifies that pupils are putting together their knowledge of what an author is saying, with how the author is using language, with who the author is writing for. Thus understanding the purpose of authors is very important as readers try to understand a range of genres of books.

It was the rare response from 1st-year secondary school less able readers which fell into this category. 'They're both sort of science experiments; they're written in the same way telling you what to do. It's actually explaining what you've got to do and things and telling you what you need and how you've got to do it.'

If we have this kind of understanding, then we appreciate, however implicitly, something about the interactive way in which language works. The fact that the junior school readers did not appreciate authors' detailed purposes suggests that they were not really independent readers – a very important observation, for, if this is the case, then we must continue to teach reading to all pupils throughout the junior school and into the secondary school. Most junior school readers probably are not really independent readers of a range of genres. Thus the secondary school cannot anticipate an intake of pupils who can be considered independent readers. These young readers will require support as they cope with more advanced reading across the curriculum. In fact, of the readers who took part in this research, it was only some average and able 4th-year secondary school readers who seemed to be reconstructing authors' meaning for themselves, as Figure 7 shows.

A 4th-year average secondary school pupil who described a technology book illustrates awareness of authors' purposes.

> That's hard. If there was a category, I'd put it between the facts and the teaching. Because it's telling you how to do something and it's also giving you answers to a certain extent.

A 4th-year secondary school able reader discussed the purpose of a science book.

> This one's got headings as well. It's got diagrams which have got headings. It

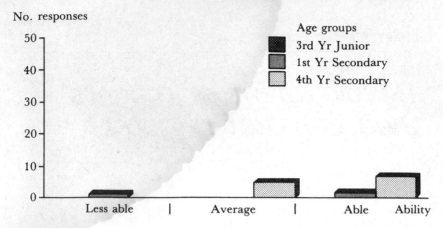

Figure 7: Readers note detailed authors' purposes

also seems to be telling you information rather than actually giving you instructions or something. Well, it's telling you about the inside of the body, it's not setting you a project like open heart surgery!

Because these pupils were aware of authors' purposes, they were becoming independent readers of a range of writing which they inevitably met in the different genres of books. In other words, independent readers have developed considerable awareness that authors of particular genre forms express meaning in particular ways but, on the basis of this research, we cannot expect the majority of pupils to reach this stage until towards the end of compulsory schooling. This must be linked to pupils' developing ability to conceptualize and thus to understand more abstract writing.

Summary

The research suggests that awareness of register of written texts is developmental. This development seems to be an important factor in learning to read, for a striking characteristic of able readers, in both junior and secondary schools, seems to be their awareness of the different features of register. Most important of all is awareness of authors' purposes. Readers seem to note the content area and then, as this becomes an implicit awareness, they continue to note other interactive aspects of register. Thus we can now consider this continuum of development in more detail.

CHAPTER 6

Development of readers' awareness of register

The development of register awareness described in this chapter is related to pupils' reading ability rather than to age, for there is no research which has established the age at which pupils ought to be capable of levels of language competency. Many of the following observations refer to pupils at different stages of their school careers but there is always reference to their ability level which is of the greatest importance.

Also, we cannot say that because a reader displays a certain awareness of the register of one type of writing, he or she is capable of the same level of awareness when reading another type of writing. Thus we should no longer try to assess readers as they read a single genre of writing. We should assess their competency as they read a range of types of writing. It would, in fact, be possible to record a profile of a pupil's awareness of register of different genres. Given time, a teacher could set a pupil a similar matching task to the one described in Chapter 5, or use a *register break* activity also described in Chapter 5.

So the description of this continuum shown in Table 3 is general; it simply indicates the order of the stages at which readers seem to become increasingly aware of register.

The stages of development

Little response to language

Some young readers taking part in the survey simply saw the task as some kind of problem-solving activity. They did not consider the task as one concerned with reading. The task might have consisted of any kind of items which had to be grouped together. Thus the responses of these pupils suggest that they looked at the pages as items to be matched in some way without looking at the way in which they were written. We are aware that many children arrive in school with little familiarity with the kind of language used in school.

Bernstein (1971) drew our attention to the differences in children's experience of language in their own environment. He described those who used a *restricted code* as only including the immediate context in their spoken language and on non-verbal ways of communication such as gesticulations. *Elaborated code* users he described as speaking in a range of ways which include speaking in an abstract sense about things outside of the immediate context. Bernstein refuted accusations that he was describing class differences in the way language is used. Unfortunately, some children began to be described as having a deficit language knowledge. We should be clear that these ideas are to do with language difference rather than language deficit. The problem for teachers is that an elaborated code is much nearer to the language of reading and writing and, therefore, of education.

Table 3   Stages of development of register awareness

Stage 1	> Stage 2	> Stage 3
reader has little response to the language	reader has some awareness of the content (field)	reader has more positive awareness of the content (field)
Stage 4	> **Stage 5**	> **Stage 6**
reader has some awareness of: how language is used (mode), who language is for (tenor), the writer's purpose	reader has more complex awareness of field, mode, tenor writer's purpose	reader is aware of the writer's purpose and how language is used to achieve this

Brice-Heath (1983) has further pointed out the difficulties which children may face in school if their experience of ways of communication differs from that of the school. She studied coloured and white working-class areas of Roadville and Tracton in the USA. Children from both these communities were less successful than the children from the more 'professional' area of the town. In fact, it seemed that the more integrated the community, the fewer formal forms of language were used.

Research, such as that of Labov (1969), argued that people who used less elaborate forms of language are able to conceptualize perfectly well. None the less, we must be concerned about the particular way in which pupils have to communicate if they are to be successful in school. We may very well over-estimate the speed at which some children respond to the language of school. In Great Britain, Wells (1985) has described linguistic difficulties which some children may experience when they enter school.

Pupils in this research who saw no relevance to language in the activity given to them were not considered non-readers. Indeed, they were children coming towards the end of the 3rd year of the junior school! We should be careful not to assume that all older junior children are equally familiar with the language used in reading and writing.

Some awareness of content

It is perhaps not surprising that young readers seem to become aware of the text itself by looking at illustrations. Even this kind of awareness seemed problematic for some 3rd-year less able junior school readers who were unable to relate illustrations to the text and who simply guessed the reason for illustrations appearing on a page. It would seem that some less able readers might benefit from specific teaching that text and illustrations should relate to each other. Sadly, some books will be found where this is not the case.

There seems to follow an awareness of individual words or groups of words. Again we may over-estimate the degree to which less able readers in the junior school are aware of continuous text. We should read continually to young pupils so that they will learn, 'how the book works, how the story goes' (Meek 1988: 7). We should also read non-fiction to pupils, particularly non-fiction which is concerned with their interests. Many information books contain lists which can be shown and read to young pupils and their purpose talked about. At this stage, there should be little explicit teaching, but considerable attempt to raise the awareness of pupils of the various ways in which texts are organized. In this way, we can help readers to become more aware of the language used by writers.

At the beginning of this book, I observed that reading is a search for meaning and not a decoding exercise. Most teachers know this and encourage their pupils to understand as they read. The first stage in understanding meaning is to be aware of the content area of the text. Thus, as pupils read for meaning, they look for the content area of the writing. However, we must remember that this is just one factor in becoming aware of the full meaning of a text.

More positive awareness of content

As readers become more confident, they seem to develop awareness of the overall content area of a text. In the research, it was noticeable that some readers incorrectly described what the text was about. Again, as teachers, we cannot assume that all pupils know what a text is about. This becomes even more important as readers cope with more formal texts in the secondary school curriculum.

It may not be surprising that so many 1st-year secondary school readers of all abilities looked at the content area of a page and identified it as belonging to a subject area. The reason for this new awareness is evident – these pupils were nearing the end of their first year following secondary school timetables based on subject specializations. This sudden awareness of even the 1st-year secondary school less able readers is marked as the less able 3rd-year junior school readers hardly referred to relevance to subject areas at all.

What is further striking, is that the 4th-year less able readers continued to describe pages they looked at as belonging to a subject area, whereas the average readers and able 4th-year readers, in particular, had less to say about this aspect and more to say about other features of the writers' language in a range of genres of books.

It seems then that less able readers are not very aware of features of vocabulary and grammar as they read. This suggests that the different ways in which vocabulary and grammar are used in genres other than narrative probably cause considerable problems to these readers' understanding. The limited view of register, that is of *content* only, which these pupils have could perhaps be widened by teacher intervention. For instance, at the secondary school stage, it would seem appropriate that teachers point out to pupils the ways in which subject texts are organized. In this way, pupils may be helped to comprehend and thus to learn.

Awareness of how language is used, who the author is writing for and why the author is writing

Of course, these different kinds of awareness are not separate; they must overlap. We have already seen that readers seem to look first at the content. There seems to be a stage which follows when the reader becomes gradually aware of different uses of grammar, vocabulary and other non-linguistic features, such as the kind of print, technical signs, etc. In the research, this stage could be identified by readers' brief and rather simplistic comments about these aspects. It was the more able readers who went further and indicated something of the purpose of the writers.

Less able 3rd-year junior school readers did not really describe features of language of the pages they reviewed. Interestingly though, less able 1st-year secondary school readers did discuss some language features of the pages they reviewed. This suggests that there is development of register awareness. Again, this further suggests that we could give slower readers more positive help in noting writers' choices of vocabulary and grammar for, as we observed at the beginning of the book, young readers do not become competent readers simply by becoming older.

More complex awareness of register

Some average and able 4th-year secondary school readers were able to make responses which suggested that they were becoming aware of the ways in which more complex features of vocabulary and grammar interact. Pupils who are able to describe what they were reading in this way were able to speak in an increasingly abstract manner. Perhaps the more pupils are able to conceptualize and articulate abstract thinking, the more explicitly aware they are of register. Here is unity of linguistic and cognitive aspects of language.

If readers are to understand different types of writing, they must have a reasonably clear idea of the writer's purpose so that they can match or compare their own purpose with that of the writer. Teachers might assist the understanding of many readers at all stages of development by discussing something about the purpose of a writer and how he or she has set about achieving it.

Whilst many readers in this research were aware of the obvious purpose of writers, it was only a few able and average 4th-year secondary school pupils who really described writers' purposes in greater detail. These pupils are well on the way to appreciating the way in which language expresses meaning, for they are recreating the meaning of the writing for themselves. They are, in other words, becoming autonomous learners which must be the real aim of education.

Summary

Pupils' awareness of register is related to their development as readers and not to their chronological age. They seem first to become aware of the field, or content of a piece of writing; then of mode, or how authors use language as they construct their writing; and then of tenor, or the formality with which authors write. As pupils come to realize the interactive way in which these features of register work, they also begin to understand that authors use language in particular ways to suit particular purposes.

Teachers can take opportunities to intervene and help young readers to become increasingly aware of why and how authors make linguistic choices. In this way, their pupils' knowledge of the ways in which different types of writing are composed will be increased with consequent benefit for their development as readers.

CHAPTER 7

Towards a continuous reading policy

Pupils continue to develop their reading ability throughout their school lives and even, we might say, in adult life for as Kress (1985) points out, more adults are readers then writers. We have realized for some time that pupils should be taught higher reading skills such as prediction and sequencing of the meaning within a text, as well as skills of information retrieval. These kinds of activities have taken place within junior schools. In many secondary schools, further teaching of reading has been limited to those pupils who have reading difficulties. It is obviously important that we develop a reading policy which is just as relevant to the secondary school as it is to the junior school.

The proposals for the National Curriculum for teaching reading to pupils from 5 to 16 years (*English for Ages 5 to 16*) state a single reading attainment target, as we have already seen. But the explanations of the levels of this single reading target contain very little description of the skills and knowledge needed by pupils if they are to read flexibly and effectively. Certainly, we can no longer argue that pupils become sufficiently aware of a range of types of writing as they extend their reading throughout their school careers. It is a major problem for all teachers to know how to intervene helpfully as their pupils of various abilities read different types of text for different purposes.

Register as an important factor in a reading policy

Knowledge of how register works can give us a key to solving something of this difficulty. We have established that various types of writing represent the individual purposes of authors who express particular meanings. Some authors wish to write narrative; others wish to give information. If young readers are to achieve the aims of the reading profile, they will have to know how individual types of writing are organized and further, as the secondary school recommendations state, 'analyse through a variety of approaches, the form and style of a writer as the method of conveying meaning'. (*English for Ages 5 to 16*, DES, 1989: 16.13).

For inexperienced readers, a range of writing may contain many problems. There is the difficulty of an unfamiliar way of writing and there is the reader's own concept of the reading process. Reading is about recreating the meaning of a text for ourselves, yet all too often younger and/or poorer readers simply decode. Somehow these readers have interpreted reading in a way which concentrates on the mechanical aspects of reading more than would a mature reader.

It is important for us to understand that different types of text cannot be distinguished solely on the basis of subject matter. It is more likely that a particular way of writing and of presenting information represents a certain way of thinking. Pupils have to be encouraged to develop reading skills which go beyond noting the subject matter into awareness of how authors use language to express meaning. Readers will not be equipped to reflect, as Bruner (1986) suggests they must, on knowledge they are given, if they do not know how that knowledge is expressed.

It seems clear that some intervention by the teacher would assist most pupils to develop their understanding of varied registers and hence their ability to read different genres of books from across the curriculum. We have already discussed some ways in which teachers can assist their developing readers without resorting to sterile teaching of language. In addition, knowledge of a range of genres of writing enables us to assess the variety of our pupils' reading across the curriculum at all stages of their school lives.

Genre balance

We know that most young pupils learn to read from narrative. They listen to stories, watch television and films and generally become very familiar with the narrative genre of writing. Stories are the usual medium for teaching reading and for enjoying reading. Imagination and fantasy are essential experiences for children's affective and emotional development. It may follow that stories are far more valued by many primary school teachers than other genres of writing and their pupils may not really experience reading or hearing other types of writing.

Later in their school careers, children will meet an increasing number of books whose registers differ from that of the story. Pupils need to become aware of various genres reasonably early and reasonably systematically, so that this is not an *ad hoc* procedure.

Primary schools usually have the great advantage of being organized in ways that allow for integrated learning. Teachers can more easily review the overall reading progress of their pupils. It is more difficult to do this in the secondary school where reading takes place in the individual lessons of a subject dominated timetable. If pupils are to read a range of writing in a balanced way throughout their school career, then we should have some form of monitoring the genres of books they read. We need to know how much emphasis we place, at a particular stage of schooling, on the reading of certain genres.

We can monitor the reading curriculum from the moment children enter school to the end of their compulsory schooling. Even this view is insufficient for most children have experienced written language before they enter school and they will continue to do so for the rest of their lives. We have to consider how we can best utilize their existing knowledge and give them a broad enough experience of texts which will enable them to read flexibly and effectively in their personal and working lives.

Monitoring readers' experience of a range of types of writing

A balanced reading curriculum can be shaped if teachers monitor the range of genres read, or *genre balance* of the reading curriculum of the school, a class, or of an individual pupil. Most certainly, this could prove to be a most effective basis for discussion between primary and secondary school colleagues as pupils prepare for the transition between schools. Discussion of this kind would make much clearer the reading demands of both schools for there will be comparison of the range of genres of writing readers have already experienced and will be expected to experience. It is essential that primary teachers understand and prepare for the reading demands of the secondary school and equally it is essential that secondary school teachers understand and build upon the reading development strategies taught in the primary school.

During my research, I looked at the reading experience of some pupils in their last primary school term and first secondary school term. The detailed results are recorded in Appendix 2. The survey revealed considerable imbalance of the genres of books read by pupils in these schools, classes and between junior and secondary schools. A worrying implication of this imbalance is that pupils entering the same secondary school may have widely varying experience of reading and therefore quite different understanding of reading.

There is considerable evidence in this survey of the large number of procedural books read. There would have been a greater emphasis had worksheets and workcards used by the pupils been taken into account. Further, many information books appear at first glance to be expository but they are, in fact, written in the procedural genre. This is not a problem as long as we recognize that we may be giving pupils an unbalanced range of writing to read.

However, the most worrying aspect of this brief survey is the small percentage of books in the expository genre which are noted. Most pupils seemed to read books in this genre as part of individual project work in the junior school, but they did not record many expository books in the first term of their secondary school. We may wonder whether these pupils gain sufficient early experience of this genre of writing. There was more evidence of reference books in the pupils' junior school booklists than in their secondary school booklists. Probably this reflects the difficulty of many secondary school pupils who move from room to room and cannot possibly keep all their books in their possession.

Surveys of this type can make clear the general book provision we are able to make for pupils. One HMI report (1988) notes that they found good provision of books in only one-tenth of the schools in England. Ingham (1986) points to financial problems which lead to a lack of books particularly in the early years of the secondary school.

A simple method of surveying the range of different types of books, or genre balance read by pupils is to:

1. List all books used by a pupil(s) across the curriculum at a particular time using a similar format to that shown in Table 4.
2. Categorize the books into genres by deciding the main purpose of the author. Authors' main purposes are shown in Table 5.
3. Compare and observe genres read by individuals, a class, even a school.

How we can help pupils to become flexible readers

If pupils are to become flexible, competent readers as the proposed reading curriculum for the National Curriculum suggests, then we have to make sure that not only their experience of different types of writing is wide, but that our teaching is informed. It seems that pupils' awareness of the registers of written language is learned from their experience of the way in which language varieties are used both in school and in everyday life. However, the responses also suggest that pupils have few strategies which help them to recognize different registers.

Although there is evidence from Australia that even very young pupils are able to discuss language features of different genres, many teachers

Table 4 A format to list the genre balance of books

Name of pupil or group			
Class			
Age			

Number of books read

Literary	*Expository*	*Procedural*	*Reference*

Totals

Percentage
of total
books

Table 5 Writers' purposes

Purpose	*Genre*

1. to narrate
    to describe personal/vicarious experience
    to use language creatively
	LITERARY

2. to describe/explain objectively
    to inform
    to discuss/argue
    to persuade
	EXPOSITORY

3. to give instructions to initiate activities	PROCEDURAL
4. to provide sequential information to provide easily referenced information	REFERENCE

would probably emphasize an approach which Brian Cambourne (1989: 48) has described as *immersion*. By *immersion*, he means that we can introduce pupils to various genres of books by 'demonstration, response, individual reading, sharing discussion, retelling'. He describes in some detail a long term method of teaching junior school pupils about different registers by discussing some reading or writing of a particular genre and by demonstrating reading and writing strategies.

Previously, we have not really taken notice that pupils who learn to read initially without too many problems may have difficulty when they read a range of genres of books. Yet, such difficulties are common. This is not really surprising when we remember that these readers are meeting language which is more formal and complex than the familiar language of stories.

This caution should not prevent us from encouraging readers in the junior school to become familiar with a range of registers of written language. Indeed, some actual teaching about more obvious register features of language may well be helpful to many junior school readers. One approach is that of *instructional scaffolding* described by Applebee and Langer (1984: 183). Here the teacher notes the difficulties of a text, and devises strategies which will help the pupils appreciate the way a text is written. The idea is that the teacher asks questions and models different forms of text as pupils work at a task which is concerned with understanding the complete text.

The context in which reading takes place is of the greatest importance. Kingman (DES 1988a: Part 2 (i)) pointed out that, 'writers and speakers adapt their language to the context in which the language is taking place'. In many schools, young writers are encouraged to become aware of the importance of context. We can also bring this awareness into the reading process. We do not read passively, for we bring to our reading our own knowledge, experiences and feelings and we then interact with the text. We can help pupils to read in this dynamic way if we discuss with them writers' purposes and attitudes and compare them with their own.

Gray (1987: 35) describes contexts for learning where 'the child is capable of functioning jointly with an adult'. Gray suggests that scaffolding activities must be introduced over a period of time until the pupil becomes a competent, independent reader who is familiar with varied texts. This is the time to introduce more difficult reading material so that pupils' learning becomes more decontextualized and therefore more independent.

This suggestion recalls the 'zone of proximal development' described by Vygotsky (1962). We should always look beyond the stage we believe the pupil to be at in order to help that pupil reach a more advanced stage. Our skill as teachers is called upon to estimate just how far we can place that goal.

Topic work

We have noted that little help is given to teachers by the proposals for the National Curriculum in reading. There are no helpful strategies proposed to assist pupils manage effective study reading. Yet, they are to learn, 'how to respond to the way information is structured and presented so that they are able to identify key points' (DES 1989: 16.39ii).

Junior school pupils usually become introduced to reading for information as they undertake topic work. A great deal has been written about topic work: many methods have been described but there has been little reference to the possible difficulties of the language which pupils read as they research, or the complexities of the language which they will use as they write or speak about their research. We have to remember that not all readers are able to read more formal writing as well as they are able to read narrative.

Awareness of language itself is just as important an aspect of topic work as the gathering of information. If we, as teachers, become concerned with *how* information is expressed as well as *what* information is given, we may assist many pupils, both in junior and secondary schools, to develop skills of reading for information and also skills of writing about the information they have researched.

Topic work involves interactive reading and writing skills. As readers write different types of writing, they become involved in creating different genres by using similar strategies as the authors whose books they read. Conversely, the reader who reads a well-written expository book is more likely to have some idea of how to compose a piece of expository writing. As Margaret Meek (1988: 36) says, 'It's the writing that makes me aware of what I'm doing when I read.'

Write it in your own words

Sometimes pupils are given a choice of topics to be researched or, perhaps more particularly in the secondary school, a specific subject to be researched. When we present these tasks to pupils, we expect that they will be able to extract information from various sources and then to reorganize that information and rewrite it. We caution them to 'write it in your own words' without perhaps realizing the difficulty of the task we are setting them.

An awareness of register informs us that whilst the books may all be concerned in some way with the same topic, they display very different kinds of language. Reading for information tasks are not simply to do with locating information, of being able to use lists of contents or indexes, but they are also ones of understanding something of how the writer has expressed meaning.

As pupils begin topic work, we can make them more aware of the different types of writing they will read. We can alert readers to the register which an author has chosen. We may be able to point out that because an author is describing dinosaurs, he or she has to use language in ways which are not as familiar as the ways in which stories are written. If we have previously read to those children descriptions and explanations, then we have helped them to become familiar with more formal registers without necessarily involving them in a formal study of language.

By asking pupils to discuss the information they have gleaned from books, we give them the opportunity to develop and clarify their thoughts. At the same time, we should be aware that the registers of spoken language are very different from those of written language. Later, we may well ask pupils to write about the information. This new task involves the writing of explanations and descriptions which, as we have noted in some detail, does not usually have the same register features as those that pupils will probably have used when they discussed their work. Thus the suggestion that pupils write the information in their own words is not really what the teacher means.

Writing about information gleaned from books can be a very difficult task. We have already noticed that expository writing usually contains some abstract language. Abstract language is not usually found in children's conversation. Writers of information books may also introduce sentences in a complex way which is certainly not part of children's speech. Yet, we are asking children to read the unfamiliar register patterning of expository text and to rewrite it in their own language. That is, we are asking them to translate possible abstraction and certain complexities of language into a register which is more familiar to them.

Consider this sentence: 'But mostly the direction of currents is affected by the spinning of the Earth' (Jennings 1988). Perhaps the sentence would be clearer like this: 'The Earth spins and helps to direct the way in which currents flow.' If you think that the original sentence could have been simplified more efficiently, try to produce your own version and then reflect upon the task which we so often give to pupils, 'write it in your own words and not those of the book'.

Pupils read more formal, unfamiliar registers in most information books. It is little wonder that they find the task of rewriting it in the same register to be a very difficult task; so difficult, in fact, that they often solve the problem of copying from the book itself.

If you do further research yourself, perhaps for an extra qualification, you may at times discover that it is necessary to quote from a text book because the author has expressed an idea so coherently that to use your own words would be to lose some of the meaning. Are not children in the same position and should we not teach them how to quote appropriately from a book?

Reading in the secondary school

The secondary school has an active part to play in continuing pupils' reading development. Yet there has appeared to be little time for reading instruction in the secondary school. Secondary school teachers often note that pupils cannot read subject text books. Some research such as that of Lunzer and Gardner (1979) suggested that secondary school pupils read for only very short periods and, in fact, they described an average 'reading burst' as 30 seconds! We might ask ourselves how far this situation has improved since that research.

Intervention in secondary school pupils' reading should be more than just a concern for less able readers but for all readers. Perhaps the process of becoming independent users of language is more evident in writing than in reading. We can, however, look for ways of intervening in the reading process which will encourage critical reading rather than just interpreting the literal sense of a text. Kress (1986) suggests that the process of reading is just as dynamic as that of writing. The written word is very powerful and we must have the ability to recreate the meaning for ourselves rather than taking the opinion as given by the writer. Competent readers make their own judgements as they read sometimes in spite of the writer's intentions. So if we teach pupils something about how writers achieve meaning in a variety of genres, we are helping them to become critical readers.

Teaching flexible reading skills is not the sole burden of the English teachers. Subject-specialist teachers have particular responsibility, for inevitably they are familiar with the language of their speciality. However, it may be that they are so familiar with the way in which their subject is written about that it is difficult for them to see language as a problem. We have already seen that subject-specialist writing cannot be ignored because these genres of writing represent the meaning of areas of learning. As Joan Rothery (1984: 107) states, 'Coming to grips with new fields generally involves coming to grips with new languages.'

Kress (1985) suggests the more academic the genre, the greater the inflexibility of the form of writing seems to be. This is probably because these genres are the means of expressing precise thinking. We might then consider the difficulty of writing worksheets for our pupils to read, for when we translate technical writing into simpler forms we may all too easily lose meaning.

This task of teaching about how language is used may well pose a major problem for secondary school teachers because they have to help pupils to understand abstract and technical language. The importance of this teaching has to be emphasized, for education comes to depend on these registers. If subject teachers are to confront this problem, they have to be able to describe the linguistic complexities of the language of their subject areas reasonably explicitly so that they can play a constructive role in developing pupils' reading.

There have been helpful teaching strategies proposed which are concerned with the linguistic construction of texts. We have already looked at scaffolding activities. *Directed Activities Related to Text* (or *DARTS*) were developed by the Nottingham University Reading or Learning Project (Davies and Greene 1981). Some activities encourage pupils to analyse the content or language of a particular text. Other activities help pupils to reconstruct a text which has been altered in some way.

There is then need for discussion with pupils about the kind of linguistic complexities discussed in Chapter 3. It may be helpful to pupils if subject teachers gradually begin to speak to pupils in more formal, subject-orientated registers. In this way, there will be some modelling of subject registers and some encouragement for secondary school pupils to discuss and read and write about the subject in a form which is close to the meanings of the subject. Barnes (1976) urged that pupils express meanings in their own terms and, of course, such a stage is essential for pupils' understanding. There may, however, be considerable value in encouraging secondary school pupils to listen to more formal language as they develop and express their own thinking and, therefore, become more familiar with this formal language.

The interaction of language and thinking has been re-emphasized by Margaret Donaldson (1989: 24) who has observed that 'thinking itself draws great strength from literacy'. She describes the kind of thinking which is usually concerned with our own experiences. Once it is detached from our personal concerns, it becomes impersonal and is, indeed, similar to more formal written language. Such written language Donaldson describes as 'the language of systematic thought' (1989: 25) as she argues the importance of young readers increasing their familiarity with more formal written language.

Summary

Knowledge of register features can provide the basis for a continuous teaching of reading policy in the junior and secondary school. The work can start in the infant classroom where children are given the opportunity to become familiar with a variety of language expression. It continues as pupils become capable readers and as they begin to read for information and to study specialist subject texts. Intervention in reading at these stages is not the sterile teaching of inert written structures. Rather, the skill of the teachers will decide to what extent this knowledge will be taught explicitly in context to pupils, or to what extent they will enhance pupils' appreciation of the link between language variety and meaning as they read. In particular, knowledge of register can inform teachers of the difficulties faced by pupils as they read for information and then write about that information.

There is evidence of imbalance in pupils' reading of different genres. Assessment can be made of the range of genres which are read at different stages of school and of general book provision.

CHAPTER 8

Value for teachers of a genre-based view of language education

The main linguistic ideas within this book relate to a *genre-based* view of language education because it provides teachers with a basis for teaching language, and, in particular, reading at every stage of schooling.

My brief research and the evidence of teacher educators in Australia suggests that, whilst teachers are implicitly aware of the way in which language works, many teachers have difficulty in describing language explicitly. I found that when a written register was seen as rather difficult, most teachers I met during this research suggested that they would only give the book in question to able readers. This response was consistent whether the teachers taught in junior or secondary school. We must then ask how less able readers are to gain understanding of more formal registers? Surely, at some stage, most readers have to be taught how to approach these registers?

Work already under way in Australia indicates very strongly that a genre-based view of language teaching has much to offer because it provides a highly practical method of describing language. Both Professor Halliday and Dr Hasan use the terms 'register' and 'genre' inter-changeably and, indeed, many people do likewise. On the other hand, some genre theorists consider genre to be linguistically superordinate to register and, therefore for them, the two terms have independent meanings.

The great advantage for education of viewing register and genre as separate meaning systems is that here are linguistic tools with which we can describe, compare and assess different books, pieces of writing and spoken communication. In this way, genre is seen as the all-important purpose and form of a communicative act. Register reflects the what, how and who of communications which are written or spoken and these aspects are expressed in appropriate language.

For instance, when we shop within a western culture, we have a certain purpose. We implicitly anticipate the form of our encounter in a shop. This is genre. The language which will be used by ourselves and the shop assistant will be determined by the products we wish to buy or discuss (what-field), the relationship between the people concerned and our attitudes (who-tenor) and by the way in which we use language (how-mode). This is register.

So we can look more closely at different genres of writing by describing the language features of their registers. Once we are aware of these language features, we are in a better position to increase pupils' awareness of different types of writing.

Many teachers in Australia discovered that as they used these ideas in the classroom, their pupils, even young pupils, became aware that genre forms are different and they began to talk about those differences and therefore about language. This kind of teaching does not infer that we teach about isolated linguistic features but rather that we point out linguistic relationships within a text.

In more general terms, a working knowledge of genre enables us to be in a better position to make decisions about the books we select for our pupils to read. We are more able to review whether authors have expressed their meanings appropriately. This infers that we will look beyond the attractive presentation of a book and look at the way in which it is written.

Curriculum genres

Perhaps the most significant development from genre-based language teaching is the *curriculum genre*. It was introduced by Frances Christie who describes a curriculum genre as referring

> to any teaching/learning episode which may be said to be structured and staged. It will involve participation of teachers and students in some activity which seeks to establish for the children understandings and/or tasks of various kinds. (Christie 1985b: 2)

The main purpose of a curriculum genre is to teach about the way language works within a genre rather than concentrating on pupils' cognitive response to a task. The curriculum genre involves modelling, teaching of structure, joint negotiation of text, consultation on a one-to-one basis and on a group basis. The consultation is about language rather than the pupil's personal input; it is a means of discussing with pupils the development of their language skills. Once pupils have understood the shape of a genre, then they can use it creatively and begin to understand the creative manipulation of it by others. This is hardly the teaching of sterile formulae.

Teachers are very active in a curriculum genre. They are not simply acting as rather passive facilitators; they are teaching something about expression of meaning and judging to what extent pupils are able to work more independently.

Extending more pupils' ability to use language flexibly

English teaching has been very much concerned with the personal development of individual pupils. There are many examples of impressive creative work produced by primary and secondary school pupils. We are told constantly that far too many pupils leave school ill-equipped to manage reading and writing tasks in the adult world. Most of us who have worked in secondary schools will have been aware of these pupils whose reading and writing attainment is worrying.

Ronald Carter (1988) suggests that reactionary and romantic opinion characterize debates about teaching English in Britain. One of the ways in which he sees possible development from such polarization is through the Australian work on genres and curricular genres. He describes genres as occupying

> a curricular space between reactionaryism and romanticism: between language as a creative resource and language as patterned regularity. (1988: 61)

A genre-based model of teaching language should not be seen in opposition to a personal development model. Rather, the two models can be seen as complementary. If we polarize the purposes of the two models, then we ignore the importance of a flexible approach to teaching language to pupils who inevitably have varying needs.

In Australia, there has been disagreement between those educationalists who believe that genre ideas are in direct opposition to the ideas of whole language exponents such as Donald Graves, whose work is so influential in that country. It is implicit within genre-based language teaching that the role of the teacher is to teach new strategies rather than being in a more consultative role as suggested by the conferencing ideas of Graves. Teaching pupils and pupils consulting with teachers are surely two sides of the same coin. The difference is in emphasis. Genre-based ideas suggest that most pupils will benefit from understanding something of the linguistic form of genres which will help them to know how to express their ideas.

Genre theory is to do with processes as well as product. Again, to polarize the two seems to waste the interactive way in which process and product can work. Language and content are dependent upon each other. To teach one without concern for the other does not seem to be reasonable.

We are suggesting that many pupils will be helped if our teaching is not solely content based. We propose that modelling forms of writing with pupils and discussing how genres are structured will assist many pupils to use language more effectively. Joan Rothery (1986) points out how much there is to be gained from teacher and pupils reconstructing the text together.

This teaching, therefore, is language based rather than content based, but the purpose of this teaching is not to inhibit expression. Pupils may well achieve greater creativity if they have some idea of the form which is appropriate for their writing. Having been introduced to forms of writing, they have the tools of the trade which they can manipulate for their own purposes.

In Great Britain, we are not yet really aware of genre-based language teaching. This may be to do with the excellent work of the Writing Research Project which has encouraged writing for different purposes. There would seem to be, however, much to be gained from a study of how we use different linguistic features as we read and write for different purposes. It should be noted, however, that there has been a study of genre (Stainton 1989) completed on behalf of the Text Types in Industry Project. The purpose of this project is to 'promote literacy skills in the world of work through the development of computer software'. It is important that we look at the relevance of teaching about genres in a wider educational context.

There are some rumbles of ensuing hot debate. Sawyer *et al.* (1989) have suggested that genre-based teaching should be approached with caution. Michael Rosen (1988) considers such teaching as imitative, and in a sense he is correct but, as we learn language, we imitate and we learn to use language creatively for our own needs.

As teachers we are involved in introducing pupils gradually to the ways in which language makes meaning in our culture. Bereiter and Scardamalia (1987) refer to *high literacy*. This kind of literacy they see as characteristic of an elitist education in Europe and the USA where its purpose has been to develop linguistic and verbal reasoning abilities. *Low literacy* they describe as the necessary literacy skills taught to the majority of people which allow them to function in the workforce in society. We want people to be capable of more than just functioning in adult life. We must be very clear that in teaching children to become familiar with a variety of texts, we are probably not only extending their linguistic flexibility but also their ability to cope with adult life.

Although pupils learn implicitly many ways of communication within our culture, not all pupils leave school being able to cope with the formal ways of adult communication. Pupils who can read the language of instruction, explanation or argument are more likely to succeed in education. In addition, they will also be more able to cope with the language used by official organizations, used by people such as bank managers, solicitors, building society officials, local council and government publications – in fact, with the kind of language which will influence their lives.

As pupils proceed through school, they are increasingly expected to produce appropriate forms of writing for different purposes and to read increasingly varied types of texts. The pupil who can understand how meaning is created persuasively, argumentatively, and descriptively is advantaged.

Christie (1985a) argues that the important purpose of teaching genres is to enable pupils to participate fully in their social environment. Once they are able to understand and manipulate the established ways of constructing meaning, then they will be in a position to express their individuality and to be creative as they go through life. Not to be able to handle genres of spoken and written communication means that they will be unable to communicate effectively.

There is the question of who decides what is appropriate as Harold Rosen (1988) asks in his response to Kingman. There is no consensus about why certain generic forms should be used for purposes of government and therefore of power. We may object to the seemingly arbitrary nature of genres but we cannot ignore their influence, for this is the way in which society works. Educators may wish to challenge them. Certainly, we wish to produce thinking, questioning adults but if challenge is to be made, it is far more effectively done from an informed position. Presumably, writers such as Joyce and Cummings knew the accepted form of the novel and poetry before they produced their own highly original work.

There may be much that we do not like and that we consider unfair in our society but both teachers and pupils need to know something of how language is used before we can speak of greater opportunity or more satisfying educational processes. As Jim Martin (1986b: 42) suggests, 'Intervention is challenging and political – it is a responsibility.'

A closer look at register and genre

Systemic-functional linguists

The work of these linguists is very relevant to a discussion which concerns how pupils read all types of text, for systemic linguists set out to describe how and why language changes as it responds to a particular social context. This is a broad view of language which looks at the way meaning is communicated rather than at language itself.

Thus systemic linguists are concerned to describe the system and the structure of linguistic communication within the social environment. They describe three main *levels of language*: substance, form and situation (Berry 1977).

The *substance* of language is either graphic or phonic, that is it is either written or spoken. The *form* of language is vocabulary and grammar. Both vocabulary and grammar are patterned in particular ways. The *situation* is where language is used. This situation is divided into the thesis or general situation, immediate situation in which language is being used, and the wider situation which encompasses the language backgrounds of the participants.

The system is established because there are relationships between the levels. Thus, phonology and graphology relate vocabulary and grammar, whilst context relates vocabulary and grammar to the situation. Each level, therefore, is able to interact. Thus we communicate through sound and writing.

Halliday is a leading systemist. He (1978) has referred to language as *social semiotic*. This term describes the relationship of language to the social context in which it is used. Individuals express meaning through language and as they do so, they create and recreate social reality.

Semiotics has been defined as 'the scientific study of the properties of signalling systems, whether natural or artificial' (Crystal 1985: 275). In this way, language can be thought of as a signalling system or a 'semiotic system' such as 'music, eating, clothes, dance' (Crystal 1985: 276). Halliday is interested in the patterns of linguistic signs to the social context of our environment. He (1985) notes that his view is a modification of that of the Greek Stoic philosophers, who studied *semainon* and *semainomenon*, and of that of Saussure who studied semiotics at the beginning of this century.

Sometimes, systemists refer to the *meaning potential* of language. The meanings that a person could make in a situation are related to the things that he or she could say. Systemists want to show how meaning and language are related. In other words, they want to show how language expresses meaning. Thus systemic thinking is more concerned with sociological linguistics than with psycho-linguistics.

Systemists are not so concerned with the mechanical aspects of language but with what language can do, or rather, with what the speaker or writer can do with language. They are concerned with the *function* of language, which is to do with the function of language in our lives. In other words, systemists are very much concerned with language and its context.

Language and context

The term *context* has several meanings. In language teaching, we are familiar with one use of *context* where it refers to language which precedes and which follows a section of text. In linguistics, however, the word *context* is used differently. Here *context* refers to the effect upon language of different situations or contexts. This has been a subject which has interested linguists for some time.

Some 50 years ago, J.R. Firth (1890–1960) held the first Chair of Linguistics in a British University. Firth saw that if we are to understand the meaning of language, we must also understand the situation or context in which it is used. Firth's thinking was greatly influenced by his colleague, Malinowski who was an anthropologist whose major research was undertaken in the Trobriand Islands in the South Pacific. As an able linguist, he learned to communicate with the islanders in their own language. Problems arose, however, when he tried to translate his conversations which proved unintelligible outside the culture of the islanders. Malinowski (1922) found it necessary to describe the cultural significance of the islanders' way of spoken expression. He used the term *context of culture* as well as *context of situation* to describe these influences on language in use.

Most significantly, Malinowski established that the most important aspect of language is its function. That function must inevitably be within a social situation because language is communicated to others. Further, Malinowski pointed out that the social situation is itself part of a context of culture. In other words, we use language within a culture but, more specifically, within a certain situation. This means that we have to appreciate the purpose of a speaker or writer and the situation in which the communication took place before we can really understand meaning fully.

On the whole we act in a way which is culturally acceptable for our purpose. If we do not, then we are considered deviant or free-thinking or even maverick. We follow the dictates of our culture but it is important to understand that by interpreting those dictates, we continue the practices of our culture and probably develop them.

Another linguist studied the way in which language plays a part in social activities. Mitchell was a former colleague of Firth who studied the language of buying and selling in a Bedouin market place in a small Cyrenaican village in what is now Libya. Mitchell was interested in the different ways in which language works in this particular situation. He studied market auctions, market transactions and shop transactions within this Arab culture and he established that language was being used in very consistent ways as the different marketing activities took place.

It is this kind of linguistic research which Halliday, a pupil of Firth, has developed. These researchers have been interested in language in use rather than in isolation. The relevance of this work for education is that we have to be aware how language is influenced by the norms of our own culture and by our purposes as we write or speak. In this way, we may see more clearly how to teach our pupils to communicate appropriately.

Register

We have already seen that register is an abstract concept. It refers to the way in which writers and speakers are able to make their language appropriate to their purpose and to their situation.

A register is a language variety. Perhaps the clearest example of the use of language variety is that of bilingual people who use different languages on different occasions. This is hardly a modern phenomenon. Halliday *et al.* (1964) described the use of language difference during the Middle Ages when a classical form of language had to be learned for writing purposes. Similarly, many present-day continental Europeans use a local language at home but the national tongue for business and formal occasions. Scribner and Cole (1981) describe the Vai people in Africa who learn three different scripts for three language uses, each for different purposes.

The concept of register itself has been studied since the 1950s when

Reid searched for a scientific approach to the study of language. He discovered that differences of register are found in any culture which has a written language or a 'literary or religious or ritual tradition of any kind' (1956: 32).

There have been many studies which have attempted to identify different registers (Halliday *et al.* (1964), Catford (1965), Davies (1969), Ellis and Ure (1969)) Halliday has continued to analyse register and it is his description which, in general, is now accepted.

Field, mode and tenor

Again, Halliday, like some earlier linguists, is concerned with the situation in which language is used. He explains that language is used for different purposes and thus different varieties or registers of language are written and spoken.

Halliday *et al.* (1964) proposed that the different situation types can be identified by a three-way classification: *field of discourse, mode of discourse, style of discourse.* Later, *style of discourse* was referred to as *tenor of discourse.* In this sense, the term *discourse* refers to the language communication concerned. Register was further defined as, 'a particular configuration of meanings that is associated with a particular situation type' (Halliday 1975: 126). This means that a type of situation or social concept can be analysed against the background of the relevant cultural situation in terms of its field, mode and tenor.

In 1985, Halliday and Hasan wrote *Language, Context and Text* as part of a series of books produced by Deakin University in Australia. These books are designed to complement courses in language education at Deakin University. They contain concise descriptions of register.

Field of discourse   In their book, Halliday and Hasan (1985: 12) describe field as referring to whatever the writer/reader or speaker/listener are concerned with. It is to do with 'the kind of social action which is taking place'. Field concerns, therefore, the content or general area of interest central to the situation.

Mode of discourse   Halliday and Hasan (1985: 12) describe mode as the part that language is playing: 'What it is that the participants are expecting language to do for them in that situation: the symbolic organisation of the text. . . .' They include in their description reference to the 'rhetorical mode, what is being achieved by the text in terms of such categories as persuasive, didactic, and the like'. This is reference to the function of the text which is the subject of debate, as we will see. Mode then concerns the way in which content is being communicated, which might be spoken or written.

In addition, Martin (1986a: 240) speaks of mode being concerned with the distance between the 'text and what it describes'. In other words, there is a certain physical distance between the communicator and the communicatee. For instance, there can be face-to-face conversation and at the other extreme, there can be a radio broadcast. The physical differences involved will influence the choice of vocabulary and grammar.

Tenor of discourse Tenor is seen as referring to the people concerned in a communication. More specifically, Halliday and Hasan (1985: 12) write of:

> –the nature of the participants, their statuses and roles: what kind of role relationship obtain among the participants, including permanent and temporary relationships of one type or another.

Tenor represents the relationship between the author/reader or the speaker/listener. This relationship could range from intimate to very formal.

Joos (1961) wrote an extremely clear description of the way in which the choice of language is affected by the relationship between the person communicating and the person listening or reading that communication. Joos used the illustration of five clocks each telling a different time to indicate that there are different ways of using English, each of which is a correct use of the language in appropriate circumstances. For instance, a mother may be speaking to her child. At the other extreme, a technical expert may be lecturing to an audience which he or she has never previously met.

Joos described the frozen language of some print, the formal language used by writers and speakers when they simply want to inform, the consultative language used when others take part in the speaking or writing, the casual language used by language participants when they know each other well, and the intimate language used when two people are expressing private meanings to each other.

The tenor also represents the attitude of the writer to the subject under consideration. The tenor of my present situation is semi-formal as I am writing for a professional audience which is unknown to me but which has an interest and probably an expertise in language in education issues. The tenor of my writing should also reflect the relevance which I believe register has for language education.

Field, mode and tenor are abstract components of any communicative context of situation. It is language which enables them to be expressed. Systemists say that register is *realized* through language. Thus there must be relationship between these aspects (field, mode, tenor) of a situation and the language used to express this communication.

Register and language

Halliday (1978) has described the main roles or functions of language in a social context.

- Language has an *ideational* function which enables us to express different kinds of content. Content may be about the physical world around us or about the inner world of consciousness and perception.
- Language has a *textual* function which enables us to actually produce the spoken or written text.
- Language has an *interpersonal* function which enables us to express our own feelings and attitudes and to reflect the relationship between ourselves and the person(s) we are communicating with.

These specific language functions can be related to the field, mode and tenor of the context of situations as follows.

Field is concerned with what is happening and is expressed through the ideational function of language. Mode is to do with the role of language and its organization and is expressed through the textual function of language. Tenor is concerned with the participants in the situation and the relationship between them and is expressed through the interpersonal function of language. This concept is represented in Table 6.

Table 6   How language reflects the context of situation

Context of situation		Language function
field (what is happening?)	(expressed through)	ideational function (expresses content)
mode (how is language used?)	(expressed through)	textual function (text production)
tenor (who is being addressed?)	(expressed through)	interpersonal function (expresses feelings and attitudes)

Thus, register allows the communicator to use language which is appropriate to the particular context of situation. To do this, the communicator makes choices from the field, mode and tenor aspects of the situation. Martin (1984) points out that there is not total freedom of choice because any situation will limit that choice. It may even be said that the writer's or speaker's choice of language is usually predictable.

For example, the writer of a science book for older secondary school readers will choose a field which is concerned with a scientific subject which will be established through use of technical language. The mode of discourse will be written. There will be considerable evidence of a cause and effect pattern of language which will necessitate the choice of certain conjunctions such as *because, although, since*. There will be many content words, complex introductions to sentences and, probably, technical signs. The tenor of discourse is likely to be formal which indicates that writers will choose to use the third person and the passive voice. So the field, mode and tenor of discourse are interactive and greatly influence the choices of vocabulary, grammar and other features.

Debate about register and genre

For some linguists, such as Halliday and Hasan, register and genre are synonomous terms, whilst other linguists have separated genre and register and see them as independent linguistic concepts.

Much of the linguistic argument centres upon the notion of *purpose*. Halliday and Hasan (1985) include function in their description of mode as previously noted. Benson and Greaves (1973) described functional tenor as the purpose for which a text was spoken and written, which influences the personal tenor. So, in their view, tenor includes a functional as well as a personal aspect.

Many genre theorists reject this view and claim that the speaker's or writer's purpose is superior to the field, mode and tenor of discourse, and, indeed, is not an aspect of register at all. Rather the purpose of the speaker or writer is seen as synonomous with genre. This means that the purpose of a speaker or writer is inextricably linked with the form (genre) of the resulting discourse. These linguists argue that the structure of a genre is not wholly accounted for by field, mode and tenor. A genre has its own identity which is determined by purpose but which is expressed through register.

For instance, the purpose of chatting amicably with a colleague is synonomous with the generic form of that conversation. The generic form of the conversation will determine the way in which it *unfolds* whilst the register will indicate what is being talked about, how it is being talked about and who the conversation is with.

This new thinking about genre is really a development of linguistic thinking about register. Martin *et al.* (n.d.: 59) point out the essential difference: 'Genre theory differs from register theory in the amount of emphasis it places on social purpose as a determining variable in language use.' In other words, the purpose of the communicator is seen to determine the form in which we speak or write, whilst register determines the choice of vocabulary and grammar etc.

Genre

Ventola (1987: 2) explains the choice of the term *genre*. She notes that literary genres are linguistic texts and that each genre is considered to be a particular type. Similarly, each genre, used in the systemic sense, has a form or structure which is expressed through register and language.

Kress (1985: 112) describes the term *genre* as, 'an attempt to capture two things: the fact that texts are [the results of] specific social events and the fact that these social events have quite specific form and function.'

Patterns of communication

In an earlier chapter it was observed that within any culture there are accepted ways of doing things which usually involve well-practised patterns of using language. In fact, it might be said that culture is a pattern of accepted ways of communicating which is continually reinforced. One of the clearest ways to demonstrate that genres have stages is to monitor the interaction with others during some kind of social encounter.

Ventola (1987: 1) describes social encounters as 'systems where social processes, which realise the social activity, unfold in stages and, in doing so, achieve a certain goal or purpose'. She continues to compare the functions of a social process to a chain. The chain has several links each with a particular function but all the links contribute to the main function of fastening the boat to the jetty. It is possible to consider social activities of all kinds in this way and to look at the links or stages which are involved in it.

Ventola further explains genre by suggesting that the term is used to distinguish between social processes which are expressed through language and those which are not such as music and dancing.

There has been considerable study of *service encounters* where someone seeks a service from another. Hasan (1978) has pointed out that we are not free to rearrange the ordering of the stages in service encounters at will, for this is dependent upon a logical way of going about things as is shown by the examples in the next paragraph.

The work of Mitchell (1957) within a Libyan culture has already been mentioned. Within our own culture, Hasan has studied patterns of communication, such as take place within a doctor's surgery (1978) and buying and selling within a market (1980). Ventola (1987) has analysed encounters within a post office, a small souvenir/jewellery/gift shop and a travel agency.

Ventola (1987: 3) a service encounter in a post office

Server: yes please (rising tone)
      (customer turns to server)

Customer: six stamps please
(server gets stamps and server hands the stamps over to the customer)
Server: a dollar twenty
(customer hands over a $20 note to server)
Server: thank you
twenty dollars
(server gets the change)
Server: it's a dollar twenty
that's . . . two four five ten and ten is twenty
thank you
Customer: thanks very much

Ventola (1987: 15) points to the structure within this verbal exchange. There is an offer of service, a request for service, a transaction, a salutation. All service encounters do not follow this pattern. For instance, bidding at an auction follows a different pattern. However, most encounters in shops in a western culture broadly follow this structure.

These studies illustrate the theory that communicative acts are implicitly organized in particular ways; they are not conducted in some sort of ad hoc manner for they have a purpose and a form. The way we communicate in these situations is obviously not rigid but we are implicitly aware of some kind of order of events. Ventola (1987: 1) explains: 'social encounters are systems where social processes, which realize the social activity, unfold in stages and, in doing so, achieve a certain goal or purpose.'

The examples just quoted are situations which involve spoken language. In Chapter 1, different forms of writing were referred to as genres. Thus genres may refer to forms of spoken or written language.

At this point, this description of a genre suggests that all texts belonging to one genre must have the same structure. However, this is not so: there is far more flexibility than this. Hasan (1978 and 1980) has described the obligatory factors which give a pattern of communication its identity. These obligatory factors are those without which a genre would lose its identity. Thus there is an accepted structure of a letter in that we greet our addressee and take leave as the letter is finished. Hasan also describes optional factors which authors or speakers may choose to use. Thus we will not write stereotyped letters. Each letter will have a slightly different purpose which will be expressed through the introduction of appropriate optional factors.

Genre, as described by Martin *et al.* (n.d.: 59), is 'a theory of language use'. It has independent meaning which indicates purposeful social activity within a culture. In this sense, genre is abstract. Ventola (1987: 85) refers to genre, register and language as, 'semiotic communication planes', that is, each plane has independent meaning but all the planes are related to each other as is illustrated in Table 7.

Table 7   Genre, register and language

GENRE or writers'/speakers' purposes

GENRE STRUCTURES or forms

REGISTER

reflected by field, mode and tenor of the context

expressed through

LANGUAGE (choices of vocabulary and grammar etc.)

Genre theory is concerned to emphasize that language makes meaning; that language and meaning are interactive, which suggests that it is difficult to separate the two. Genre, therefore, is a most significant linguistic factor. Jim Martin (1984: 28) has described it in this way:

> For us, genre is a staged, goal oriented, purposeful activity in which speakers engage as members of our culture. Virtually everything you do involves you participating in one or other genre. Culture seen in these terms can be defined as a set of generically interpretable activities.

Social implications

Kress (1985: 99) looks at the social implications of genre:

> The category of genre captures that interconnectedness of social and linguistic forms and processes; knowledge of genre is an indispensable prerequisite for effective participation in social life.

Thus genres have social significance, for they may be considered as socio-linguistic reflections of society. It therefore follows that if pupils are to play full and effective parts within society, then they must have wide experience of different genres. Kress (1989: 143) again explains:

> Genres are intimately tied into the social, political and cultural structures and practices of a given society, and arise as expressions of certain fundamental meanings of these structures and practices.

Social events, then, have a form and a purpose. Language is used in a particular way, written or spoken, in order to express that purpose. Genres are learnt by children as they interact as members of our culture. It is interesting to reflect that as these genres are learned and used, culture is recreated and continued. Of course, the forms of genre change. Even the rigid genres of some church services gradually change as people's understandings change. In this way, they reflect social change.

Genres, therefore, can be considered as the form or shape of a spoken or written communication which are shaped in general by the norms of culture.

Inter-textuality

Inter-textuality is the notion that language users do not begin to listen or read without prior concepts which will affect their understanding. The dynamics of genre theory have resulted in further study of this concept. Kress considers that the wider context of an author has to be considered just as closely as his or her purpose for he sees that register may be constrained by more than genre.

The meaning readers reconstruct of any type of writing is necessarily influenced by other texts they have read and conversations and experiences they have had. Threadgold (1986: 24) explains, 'Different audiences will have at their disposal different repertoires of discourse.' Discourse is used here in the sense of 'knowledge, prejudices, resistances' (1986: 24). She further states that writers and readers 'are economically, politically and ideologically determined by the different access which they have to sets of discourse' (1986: 25).

The genre balance of some pupils' reading

A survey was made of the different genres of books read by some readers as they transferred from junior to secondary school.

Ninety-nine pupils in four junior school classes completed a list of the books they were using in school during their final junior school term. These pupils completed a similar list during their first term in their new secondary schools. Two of the junior schools transferred children to the same secondary school and similarly the other two junior schools transferred children to the same secondary school.

The books listed by the pupils were categorized into literary, expository, procedural and reference genres. It was then possible to compare the percentage of books listed in each genre.

Table 8 Results: survey of genres of books read by some pupils in their last junior school term.

	Schools			
	A%	*B%*	*C%*	*D%*
Literary	57.2	16.5	20.0	54.4
Expository	2.8	13.7	18.1	4.4
Procedural	26.0	52.4	47.6	41.1
Reference	13.8	17.2	14.1	0.0
Average books per child	6.3	9.6	7.0	3.0

Table 9 Results: survey of genres of books read by some pupils in their first secondary school term.

Secondary school A

	Ex-junior school A%	*Ex-junior school B%*
Literary	20.0	22.0
Expository	4.5	0.8
Procedural	70.0	73.7
Reference	5.4	3.3
Average books per child	6.1	5.9

Secondary school B

	Ex-junior school C%	*Ex-junior school D%*
Literary	44.0	45.4
Expository	10.3	14.1
Procedural	41.8	39.3
Reference	3.8	1.0
Average books per child	4.9	4.3

Register break puzzles

3rd-year junior school

Underline any part of these readings which you think is written in a different way.

From *A Hundred and One Dalmations* Smith (1957)

The dogs heard the word 'puppies', saw Nannie Cook's tears, and rushed down to the area. Then they went dashing over the whole house, searching, searching. Every few minutes, Missis and Peredita howled, and Pongo barked furiously.

While the dogs searched and the nannies <u>went bananas</u>, Mrs Dearly telephoned Mr Dearly. He came home at once, bringing with him one of the top men from Scotland Yard. The Top Man found a bit of sacking on the area railings and said the puppies must have been dropped into sacks and driven away in the black van. He promised to comb the underworld, but warned the Dearlys that dogs which had been <u>nicked</u> were seldom recovered unless a reward was offered.

From *The Saxons* Triggs (1979)

Each family owned separate strips of land but the work of ploughing was probably shared. They left a path of unploughed soil between each strip. Each year one field in every two or three was left unploughed. Animals were kept in these fallow fields. The animals' manure kept the fields fertile.

Most villages had permanent meadowland and woodland nearby. In late summer and early autumn the <u>blokes</u> mowed the meadows with scythes to make hay for winter <u>grub.</u>

From *Good Health 2* Johnson and Williams (1980)

Can you think why a baby can't start eating meals such as you eat straight away?

How does a baby tell its parents that it is hungry?

Can you find out what the next stages are in feeding a baby? Ask at home when you started:

1. eating solids
2. having <u>proper food made all sloppy</u>
3. <u>mucking about with a spoon</u>
4. and when your first teeth arrived to help you feed yourself.

From *Trees* Williams (1972)

Hawthorn

Two kinds of hawthorn are found in Britain, the common variety, and the 'midland' variety.

   The common hawthorn can be either a tree or a bush. The tree is <u>flipping</u> high and it is often planted along streets. Flowering is in May and the fruits look rather like rose-hips. Birds <u>gobble them up</u> and spread the seeds with their droppings.

1st-year secondary school

Underline any part of these readings which you think is written in a different way.

From *Thunder and Lightning* Mark (1976)

Andrew noticed several rolls of carpet stacked against the back door. None of them had fitted the last house and they had been rolled up for years. They were all off-cuts, bought cheaply in sales and they didn't look as if they would fit this house either. Mum unfurled one and took it into the garden to <u>chuck</u> on the line.

From *The Peppermint Pig* Bawden (1975)

The little front sitting room of the cottage was furnished with what was left of their London house. Most of the valuable things had been <u>flogged</u>, the grandfather clock, and the round walnut table, and the pretty Chippendale chairs, but the book case with the brass inlay and the secret drawer that flew open when you pressed a knob at the side was brought down to Norfolk, and Mother's treadle sewing machine, and the old leather sofa that had been kept in the kitchen in London because it was too shabby for the parlour.

From *The Cambridge Scene* Graham-Cameron (1977)

The River Cam, which flows through the city of Cambridge, was once much wider and surrounded by swampy land. If people or animals tried to cross they sank into the bog and sometimes drowned. But they soon discovered a place where two ridges of land come right down to the edge of the river, where they could wade across without too much danger. Gradually houses were built beside this fording place and much later, a bridge was made giving the present city its name.

To the north-east of Cambridge was a huge area of undrained fenland. It was very difficult to cross this lonely <u>mucky bit</u> as there were no known tracks.

From *Looking at Science 2* Fielding (1984)

Put a bowl of water on your desk. Press a ball of soft plasticine around one end of a plastic drinking straw. Press the plasticine into a long thin shape. Put the plasticine into the water and use the straw to move it around. See how easily it slips through the water.

<u>Have a bash</u> at pressing the plasticine into a wide flat shape. See if this moves as easily. Try it with several different shapes.

4th-year secondary school

Underline any part of these readings which you think is written in a different way.

From *Astronomy* Brown (1984)

Even Copernicus did not get his ideas about the Sun and its family of revolving planets quite right. From early Greek times it was assumed that when one body revolved about another, its path, or orbit, would always be in a perfect circle. Copernicus, too, believed this was true. <u>A chap called</u> Johannes Kepler decided this was a <u>load of rubbish.</u>

From *Science 1* Hill and Holman (1986a)

Blood has many important jobs to do. Its major function is to act as a transport system, carrying oxygen and food to all parts of the body, and carrying away waste products. To do this it <u>whips around</u> the body through a <u>load of blood vessels.</u>

The heart is a 'blood pump'. When blood leaves the heart, it is under high pressure. The vessels carrying the blood away from the heart have to withstand this pressure, so they have thick muscular walls.

From *All about Tropical Fish* McInerny and Gerard (1958)

SPOTTED BARB
Congo
Community   Diet: all foods   Swims: Lower half of tank
Similar in size and shape to *B. bimaculatus*, this newly imported barb is interesting, though not highly coloured.

The tail is black olive, the sides greyish-brown, the belly white. From gill-plate to tail a single line of dots, spaced equally apart, give the fish its name. It is <u>really shy and mucks about</u> on the top of the sand just under the low plant leaves.

From *Design and Technology* Yarwood *et al.* (1983)

With the brace at an angle of 35° to the upright of the bracket, draw triangles of force for the bracket when the following weights are hung at A: 1. 500 grams; 2. 300 grams; 3. 250 grams. Take 1 kilogram force as equal to 10 newtons and work to a scale of 25 mm as representing 1 newton.

<u>Have a go</u> at measuring how long each side of the triangle is and state the forces acting along the arm and brace in each case.

From *The Angry Mountain* Innes (1950)

It was past five when we reached the villa, by a dusty track that ran dead straight through flat, almost white earth planted with bush vines. The villa itself was perched on a sudden rise where some long-forgotten lava flow had abruptly ceased. It was the usual white stucco building with flat roof and balconies and some red tiling to relieve the monotony of the design. As the car stopped the heat <u>nearly knocked us out</u>. There was no sun but the air was heavy and stifling.

School books mentioned

Adams, R. (1972). *Watership Down*. London, Puffin.

Bawden, N. (1975). *The Peppermint Pig*. London, Puffin.

Brown, P.L. (1984). *Astronomy*. Orbis.

Burrell, R. (1988). *A First Ancient History. On the Threshold of History*. Oxford, Oxford University Press.

Carwardine, (1987). *Water Animals*. Oxford, Oxford University Press.

Children's Britannica. (1964). Wallington, Surrey, Encyclopaedia Britannica International Ltd.

Collins Gem English Dictionary (1985). London, Collins.

Concise Oxford Dictionary of Current English adapted by Fowler, H.W. and Fowler, F.G. (1950) from *The Oxford Dictionary*. Oxford at the Clarendon Press.

Cutting, B. and Cutting, J. (1989). *The Tree*. London, Sunshine Books, Heinemann Educational.

Dahl, R. (1964). *Charlie and the Chocolate Factory*. London, Puffin.

Dahl, R. (1983). *The Grand High Witch*. London, Puffin.

Day Lewis, *see* Lewis, C. Day.

Fielding, D. (1984). *Looking at Science 2: The Natural World*. Oxford, Blackwell.

Fyleman R. (1956). 'Mice,' in *Come Follow Me*. London, Evans Brothers.

Ginn Science (1988). *The Tomato Plant*. Aylesbury, Ginn.

Graham-Cameron, E. (1977). *The Cambridge Scene*. Cambridge, Dinosaur.

Greene, G (1938). *Brighton Rock*. London, Heinemann Educational.

Hart, R. (1978). *Chemistry Matters*. Oxford, Oxford University Press.

Hill, G. and Holman, J. (1986a). *Science 1*. Windsor, Nelson.

Hill, G. and Holman, J. (1986b). *Science 2*. Windsor, Nelson.

Innes, H. (1950). *The Angry Mountain*. London, Collins.

Jennings, T. (1988). *The Young Geographer Investigates – Oceans and Seas*. Oxford, Oxford University Press.

Johnson, V. and Williams, T. (1980). *Good Health 2*. Windsor, Nelson.

Leutscher, A. (1971). *Dinosaurs and Other Pre-Historic Animals*. London, Hamlyn.

Lewis, C. Day (1948). *The Otterbury Incident*. London, Puffin.

McCullagh, S. (1970). *Red Planet 2 – Adventures in Space*. London, Hart-Davis.

McCullagh, S. (1985). *Miranda and the Magic Mixture*. London, Collins Educational.

McInerny, D. and Gerard, G. (1958). *All About Tropical Fish*. London, Harrap.

McSweeney, T. and Debes, A. (eds) (1975). *Open English*. London, Longman.

Mark, J. (1976). *Thunder and Lightning*. London, Heinemann Educational.

Moorman M. (ed.) (1971). *Journals of Dorothy Wordsworth*. Oxford, Oxford University Press.

Murnane, W.J. (1983). *A Penguin Guide to Ancient Egypt*. London, Penguin.

Pluckrose, H. (1988). *Manager of a Wild Life Park*. Oxford, Oranges and Lemons, Blackwell Educational.

Pople, S. (1982). *Explaining Physics*. Oxford, Oxford University Press.

Ransome, A. (1930). *Swallows and Amazons*. London, Puffin (1962).

Smith, D. (1957). *A Hundred and One Dalmatians*. London, Heinemann.

SMP (n.d.). *11–16*, Book B3. Cambridge, Cambridge University Press.

Triggs, T.D. (1979). *The Saxons*. Hemel Hempstead, Macdonald Educational.

Turner, D. (1988). *Bread*. Hove, Sussex, Wayland.

Unstead, R.J. (1959). *Looking at Ancient History*. London, A & C Black.

Ward, B.R. (1982). *Touch, Taste, Smell*. London, Watts.

Williams, C. (1972). *Trees*. London, Black's Picture Information Books.

Wright, W.D. (1976a). *A First Encyclopaedia*. Hitchin, Nisbet.

Wright, W.D. (1976b) *A First Dictionary*. Hitchin, Nisbet.

Wykeham, N. (1979) *Machines of Today and Tomorrow: Farm Machines*. Hove, Sussex, Wayland.

Yarwood, A., Orme, A. and Orme, A.H. (1983). *Design and Technology*. Dunton Green, Sevenoaks, Hodder and Stoughton.

References

Andrews, R. (ed.) (1989). *Narrative and Argument*. Milton Keynes, Open University Press.

Applebee, A.N. and Langer, J. (1983). 'Instructional scaffolding: reading and writing as natural language activities', in Jenson, J. (ed.) (1984), *Composing and Comprehending*. National Conference on Research in English. ERIC Clearing House on reading and communication skills.

Barnes, D. (1976). *From Communication to Curriculum*. Harmondsworth, Penguin.

Benson, J.D. and Greaves, W.S. (1973). *The Language People Really Use*. Agincourt, Ontario, the Book Society of Canada.

Bereiter, C. and Scardamalia, M. (1987). 'An attainable version of high literacy: approaches to teaching higher order skills in reading and writing', *Curriculum Inquiry*, Spring, vol. 17, no. 1.

Bernstein, B. (1971). *Class, Codes and Control. Vol. 1: Theoretical Studies Towards a Sociology of Language*. London, Routledge and Kegan Paul.

Berry, M. (1977). *An Introduction to Systemic Linguistics, 2: Levels and Links*. London, Batsford.

Binkley, M.A. (1983). 'A descriptive and comparative study of cohesive structure in text materials from differing academic disciplines'. Unpublished PhD dissertation. USA, The George Washington University.

Brice-Heath, S. (1983). *Ways With Words: Language, Life and Work in Communities and Classrooms*. Cambridge, Cambridge University Press.

Bruner, J. (1986). *Actual Minds, Possible Worlds*. Massachusetts, Harvard University Press.

Cambourne, B. and Brown, H. (1989). 'Learning to control different registers', in Andrews, R. (ed.).

Carter, R. (1988). 'Some pawns for Kingman: language education and English teaching,' in *Applied Linguistics in Society*. Papers from the Twentieth Anniversary Meeting of the British Association for Applied Linguistics held at the University of Nottingham, September 1987. Centre for Information on Language Teaching and Research.

Catford, J.C. (1965). *A Linguistic Theory of Translation*, Oxford, Oxford University Press.

Chapman, L.J. (1983). *Reading Development and Cohesion*. London, Heinemann Educational Books.

Chapman, L.J. (1987). *Reading: From 5 to 11 years*. Milton Keynes, Open University Press.

Christie, F. (1985a). *Language Education*, Victoria, Deakin University.

Christie, F. (1985b). 'Curriculum genres: towards a description of the construction of knowledge in schools'. Paper presented at the working conference on: Interaction of Spoken and Written language in Educational Settings. University of New Zealand. November 1985.

Crystal, D. (1980). *A Dictionary of Linguistics and Phonetics*, Oxford, Basil Blackwell.

Davies, A. (1969). 'The notion of register', *Educational Review*, November, vol. 22, no. 1, pp. 64–77.

Davies, F. and Greene, T. (1981). 'Directed activities related to text: text analysis and text reconstruction'. Presentation to the 26th Convention of the International Reading Association, New Orleans.

Department of Education and Science (1975). *A Language for Life*. A Report of the Committee of Inquiry Appointed by the Secretary of State for Education and Science under the Chairmanship of Sir Allan Bullock FBA. London, Her Majesty's Stationery Office.

Department of Education and Science (March 1988a). Report of the Committee of Inquiry into the Teaching of English Language under the Chairmanship of Sir John Kingman, FRS. London, Her Majesty's Stationery Office.

Department of Education and Science (November 1988b). *English for Ages 5 to 11*. National Curriculum Proposals of the Secretary of State for Education and Science and the Secretary of State for Wales. London, Her Majesty's Stationery Office.

Department of Education and Science (June 1989). *English for Ages 5 to 16*. National Curriculum. Proposals of the Secretary of State for Education and Science and the Secretary of State for Wales. London, Her Majesty's Stationery Office.

Donaldson, M. (1989). *Sense and Sensibility. Some Thoughts on the Teaching of Literacy*. Occasional Paper No. 3. University of Reading, School of Education.

Doughty, P., Pearce, J. and Thornton, G. (1971). *Language in Use*. Schools Council Programme in Linguistics and English Teaching. London, Arnold.

Eggins, S., Martin, J.R. and Wignell, P. (1987). *Working Papers in Linguistics No. 5. Writing Project*. Linguistics Department, University of Sydney.

Ellis, J. and Ure, J.N. (1969). 'Registers', in Butler, C.S. and Hartmann, R.R.K. (eds) (1976), *A Reader on Language Variety*, vol. 1, Exeter Linguistic Studies. University of Exeter.

Freeman, A. and Pringle, I. (1989). 'Contexts for developing argument', in Andrews, R. (ed.) (1989).

Gray, B. (1987). 'How natural is "natural" language teaching? – Employing wholistic methodology and the classroom', *Australian Journal of Early Childhood*, December, vol. 12, no. 4.

Halliday, M.A.K. (1975). *Learning How to Mean*. London, Arnold.

Halliday, M.A.K. (1978). *Language as a Social Semiotic – The Social Interpretation of Language and Meaning*. London, Arnold.

Halliday, M.A.K. (1980). 'Context of situation and the structure of a text', in Halliday, M.A.K. and Hasan, R. (1980).

Halliday, M.A.K. (1984). 'Spoken and written modes of meaning', in Horowitz, R. and Samuels, J. (eds) (1984), *Comprehending Oral and Written Language.* London, Academic Press.

Halliday, M.A.K. (1985). *An Introduction to Functional Grammar.* London, Edward Arnold.

Halliday, M.A.K. and Hasan, R. (1980). 'Text and context: aspects of language in a social-semiotic perspective', *Sophia Linguistica,* 1980 VI. Working Papers in Linguistics. Tokyo, Sophia University.

Halliday, M.A.K. and Hasan, R. (1985). *Language, Context and Text: Aspects of Language in a Social-Semiotic Perspective.* Oxford, Oxford University Press.

Halliday, M.A.K., McIntosh, A. and Strevens, P. (1964). *The Linguistic Sciences and Language Teaching.* London, Longman.

Hasan, R. (1978). 'Text in the systemic-functional model', in Dressler, W.U. (ed.) (1978), *Current Trends in Text Linguistics.* New York, de Gruyter.

Hasan, R. (1980). 'The structure of text', in Halliday, M.A.K. and Hasan, R. (1980).

HMI (1988). *Secondary Schools – An Appraisal by HMI 1982–1986.* London, Her Majesty's Stationery Office.

HMI (December 1989). *Reading Policy and Practice at Ages 5–14. Summer 1989.* Middlesex, Department of Education and Science.

Horrowitz, R. (1985). 'Text patterns. Part 1', in *Journal of Reading,* February, vol. 28. no. 5, pp. 448–54.

Hull, R. (1985). *The Language Gap. How Classroom Dialogue Fails.* London, Methuen.

Hymes, D. (1972). 'Models of the interaction of language and social life', in Gumperz, J.J. and Hymes, D. (1972), *Directions in Socio-Linguistics.* London, Holt, Rinehart and Winston.

Ingham, J. (1986). *The State of Reading.* A Research Project of the Educational Publishers Council. London, The Publishers Association.

Joos, M. (1961). *The Five Clocks.* New York, Harcourt, Brace and World.

Kinneavy, J.L., Cope, J.Q. and Campbell, J.W. (1976). *Writing – Basic Modes of Organisation.* Dubeque, Iowa, Kendal/Hunt.

Kress, G.R. (1985). 'Socio-linguistic development and the mature language user: different voices for different occasions', in Wells, G and Nicholls, J. (1985), *Language and Learning: An Interactional Perspective.* London, Falmer Press.

Kress, G.R. (1986). 'Reading, Writing and Power', in Painter C. and Martin, J.R. (eds) (1986).

Kress, G.R. (1989). 'Texture and meaning', in Andrews, R. (ed.) (1989).

Labov, W. (1969). 'The logic of non-standard English', in *Language and Education* (1972), Language and Learning Course Team at the Open University. London, Routledge and Kegan Paul/Milton Keynes, Open University.

Littlefair, A.B. (1988). 'An exploration into pupil and teacher awareness of the register and genres of books used in school'. Unpublished PhD thesis. Milton Keynes, Open University.

Littlefair, A.B. (1990). 'Comment on Cox: the linguistic concepts of register and genre'. in Hunter-Carsch, M., Beverton, S. and Dennis, D. (eds) (1990), *Primary English in the National Curriculum*. Oxford, Blackwell.

Lunzer, E. and Gardner, K. (1979). *The Effective Use of Reading*. London, Heinemann Educational.

McLeod, J. (1970). *Gap Reading Comprehension. Form R and Form B*. London, Heinemann Educational.

McLeod, J. and Anderson, J. (1973). *Gapadol Reading Comprehension. Form Y and Form G*. London, Heinemann Educational.

Mackay, D. Thompson, B. and Schaub, P. (1970, 1978). *Breakthrough to Literacy*. London, Longman for Schools Council Programme in Linguistics and English Teaching.

Malinowski, B. (1922). *Argonauts of the Western Pacific – An Account of Native Enterprise and Adventure in the Archipelogoes of Melanesian New Guinea*. London, Routledge and Kegan Paul.

Martin, J.R. (1984). 'Language, register and genre', in ECT 418 (1984), *Language Studies. Children Writing: Reader*. Victoria, Deakin University.

Martin, J.R. (1986a). 'Intervening in the process of writing development', in Painter, C. and Martin, J.R. (eds) (1986).

Martin, J.R (1986b) 'Grammaticalising ecology: the politics of baby seals and kangaroos'. in Threadgold, T. (1986).

Martin, J.R. and Peters, P. (1983). 'On the analysis of exposition', in Hasan, R. (1983), *Discourse on Discourse*. Occasional Papers No. 7. Workshop Reports from the Maquarie Workshop on Discourse Analysis. Applied Linguistics Association of Australia.

Martin, J.R. and Rothery, J. (1981). 'The ontogenesis of written genre', *Working Project, Report 1981*. Working Papers in Linguistics, No. 2. Linguistics Department, University of Sydney.

Martin, J.R, Christie, F. and Rothery, J. (n.d.). 'Social processes in education: a reply to Sawyer and Watson (and others)', in Reid, I. (ed.) (n.d.), *The Place of Genre in Learning: Current Debates*. Typereader Publications No. 1. Centre for Studies in Literary Education. Victoria, Deakin University.

Martin, N., D'Arcy, P., Newton, B. and Parker, R. (1976). *Writing and Learning across the Curriculum 11-16*. Schools Council Project. London, Ward Lock Educational.

Meek, M. (1988). *How Texts Teach What Readers Learn*. Stroud, Gloucester, Thimble Press.

Mitchell, T.F. (1957). *The Language of Buying and Selling in Cyrenaica: A Situational Statement*. Hesperis, vol. XLIV, pp. 37-71.

Moffat, J. (1968). *Towards a Universe of Discourse*. Boston, Houghton Mifflin.

National Writing Project (1985-8). London, Schools Curriculum Development Council.

Painter, C. and Martin, J.R. (1986). *Writing to Mean: Teaching Genres Across the Curriculum*. Papers and workshop reports from the 'Writing to Mean' Conference held at the University of Sydney, May 1985.

Perera, K. (1984). *Children's Writing and Reading. Analysing Classroom Language*. Oxford, Basil Blackwell.

Perera, K. (1986). 'Some linguistic difficulties in school text books', in Gillham,

B. (1986), *The Language of School Subjects*. London, Heinemann Educational Books.

Reid, T.B.W. (1956). 'Linguistics, structuralism and philology', in *Archivum Linguisticum*, vol. 8, pt. 2, pp. 28–37.

Rosen, H (1988). 'Responding to Kingman', in *Responding to Kingman*. Proceedings of a national conference on the Kingman Report held at Nottingham University, 21 June 1988.

Rosen, M. (1988). 'Will genre theory change the world?', in *English in Australia*, December, no. 86.

Rothery, J. (1980) 'Narrative: vicarious experience', in Martin, J.R. and Rothery, J., *Writing Project, Report 1980*. Working Papers in Linguistics No 1. Linguistics Department, University of Sydney.

Rothery, J. (1984). 'The development of genres – primary to junior secondary school', in ECT 418 (1984), *Language Studies. Children Writing: Study Guide*. Victoria, Deakin University.

Rothery, J. (1986). 'Teaching writing in the primary school: a genre based approach to the development of writing abilities', in Martin, J.R. and Rothery, J., *Writing Project, Report 1986*. Working Papers in Linguistics No 4. Linguistics Department, University of Sydney.

Saussure, F. de. *Course in General Linguistics*. Translated by Baskin, W. (1974). London, Collins/Fontana. First published and edited by Bally, C. and Sechehaye, A. (1974).

Sawyer, W., Adams, A. and Watson, K. (1989). *English Teaching from A to Z*. Milton Keynes, Open University Press.

Scribner, S. and Cole, M. (1981). 'Unpackaging literacy', in Whiteman, N.F. (ed.) (1981). *The Nature, Development and Teaching of Written Communication*. New Jersey, Lawrence Erlbaum. Edited version in Mercer, N. (ed.) (1988), *Language and Literacy*, vol. 1, Language Studies. Milton Keynes, The Open University.

Stainton, C. (1989). *Report on Genre and Genre Study*. Department of English Studies, Nottingham University.

Threadgold, T. (1986). 'Semiotics, ideology, language', in Threadgold, T. *et al.* (eds) (1986).

Threadgold, T., Grosz, E.A., Kress, G. and Halliday, M.A.K. (eds) (1986). *Semiotics, Ideology, Language*. The Sydney Association for Studies in Society and Culture. Department of Anthropology, University of Sydney.

Tinker, M.A. (1963). *Legibility of Print*. Iowa State University.

Ure, J. (1969). 'Lexical density and register differentiation', in Perren, G.E. and Trim, J.L.M. (1971), *Applications of Linguistics*. Selected papers of the Second International Congress of Applied Linguistics – Cambridge, 1969. Cambridge University Press.

Ventola, E. (1987). *The Structure of Social Interaction. A Systemic Approach to the Semiotics of Service Encounters*. London, Pinter.

Vygotsky, L. (1962) *Thought and Language*. Newly revised and edited by Kozulin, A. (1986). Cambridge, Massachusetts, MIT.

Wells, C.G. (1985). *Language, Learning and Education*. Selected papers from the Bristol Study: *Language at Home and School*. Windsor, NFER-Nelson.

Wignell, P. (1987). 'In your own words', in Eggins *et al.* (1987).
Wray, D. and Medwell, J. (1989). 'Using desk-top publishing to develop literacy',
  Reading, vol. 23, no. 2 (July), pp. 62–8.

Index